Windows Server 2008 Network Infrastructure Configuration

Lab Manual

WILEY

EXECUTIVE EDITOR	John Kane
EDITORIAL ASSISTANT	Jennifer Lartz
DIRECTOR OF MARKETING AND SALES	Mitchell Beaton
PRODUCTION MANAGER	Micheline Frederick
PRODUCTION EDITOR	Kerry Weinstein
DEVELOPMENT AND PRODUCTION	Custom Editorial Productions, Inc.

To order books or for customer service, please call 1-800-CALL WILEY (225-5945).

ISBN 978-0-470-22514-1

Printed in the United States of America

10 9 8 7 6 5

BRIEF CONTENTS

1. Introducing Windows Server 2008 Networking   1

2. Installing Microsoft Windows Server 2008   14

3. Configuring and Managing the DHCP Server Role   29

4. Configuring and Managing the DNS Server Role   44

5. Configuring Routing and Remote Access (RRAS)   63

6. Configuring File Services   81

7. Configuring Print Services   99

8. Maintaining and Updating Windows Server 2008   110

9. Securing Data Transmission and Authentication   128

10. Configuring Network Health   150

11. Maintaining Windows Server 2008 File Services   167

    Troubleshooting Lab   179

CONTENTS

1. **Introducing Windows Server 2008 Networking   1**

   Exercise 1.1: Modifying Basic Server Settings   3

   Exercise 1.2: Configuring TCP/IP Settings   5

   Exercise 1.3: Configuring a Second Windows Server 2008 Computer   6

   Exercise 1.4: Configuring a Windows Server 2008 Server Core Computer (optional)   9

   Lab Review Questions   12

   Lab Challenge: Configuring the Windows Firewall   13

2. **Installing Microsoft Windows Server 2008   14**

   Exercise 2.1: Installing Windows Server 2008   16

   Exercise 2.2: Configuring Windows Server 2008   18

   Exercise 2.3: Installing and Configuring a Second Windows Server 2008 Computer   20

   Exercise 2.4: Installing and Configuring a Windows Server 2008 Core Computer (optional)   23

   Exercise 2.5: Installing and Configuring a Windows Vista Computer (optional)   26

   Lab Review Questions   27

   Lab Challenge: Joining an Active Directory Domain   28

3. **Configuring and Managing the DHCP Server Role   29**

   Exercise 3.1: Installing the DHCP Server Role   31

   Exercise 3.2: Confirming DHCP Server Functionality   33

   Exercise 3.3: Managing the DHCP Server Role   35

   Exercise 3.4: Installing and Configuring the DHCP Server Role on Server Core (optional)   39

   Lab Review Questions   40

   Lab Challenge: Authorizing a DHCP Server in Active Directory   41

   Lab Cleanup   42

4. **Configuring and Managing the DNS Server Role   44**

   Exercise 4.1: Installing the DNS Server Role   46

   Exercise 4.2: Configuring a Secondary Zone and Zone Transfers   51

   Exercise 4.3: Configuring Reverse Lookup Zones and Confirming DNS Functionality   54

   Exercise 4.4: Installing and Configuring the DNS Server Role on Server Core   58

   Lab Review Questions   60

   Lab Challenge: Configuring DNS Forwarders   60

   Lab Cleanup   61

5. **Configuring Routing and Remote Access (RRAS)   63**

Exercise 5.1: Managing the Windows Routing Table   65
Exercise 5.2: Installing the Routing and Remote Access Role   71
Exercise 5.3: Configuring Virtual Private Networking   75
Exercise 5.4: Configuring NPS Network Policies   76
Lab Review Questions   78
Lab Challenge: Working with Delayed Start Services in Windows Server 2008   78
Lab Cleanup   79

6. **Configuring File Services   81**

Exercise 6.1: Installing the File Server Resource Manager   83
Exercise 6.2: Creating and Managing Windows File Shares   85
Exercise 6.3: Configuring DFS-Namespaces   89
Exercise 6.4: Configuring DFS-Replication   91
Lab Review Questions   95
Lab Challenge 6.1: Configuring a File Screen   95
Lab Challenge 6.2: Configuring File Shares on a Server Core Computer   96
Lab Cleanup   96

7. **Configuring Print Services   99**

Exercise 7.1: Installing the Print Server Role   101
Exercise 7.2: Creating and Managing Windows Printers   102
Exercise 7.3: Installing the Internet Printing Protocol   105
Lab Review Questions   107
Lab Challenge: Publishing Printers in Active Directory Using Group Policy   107
Lab Cleanup   107

8. **Maintaining and Updating Windows Server 2008   110**

Exercise 8.1: Using the Reliability and Performance Monitor   112
Exercise 8.2: Using the Windows Event Viewer   114
Exercise 8.3: Installing and Using the Windows Network Monitor   116
Exercise 8.4: Installing and Configuring WSUS   119
Lab Review Questions   124
Lab Challenge: Creating a Computer Group in WSUS   125
Lab Cleanup   125

9. **Securing Data Transmission and Authentication   128**

Exercise 9.1: Configuring IPSec to Allow and Block Traffic   130
Exercise 9.2: Managing IPSec Authentication and Encryption Settings   135
Exercise 9.3: Configuring the Windows Firewall   139
Exercise 9.4: Configuring Connection Security Rules   142
Exercise 9.5: Configuring the Windows Firewall on Server Core (optional)   145
Lab Review Questions   146
Lab Challenge: Configuring the Remote Administration Exception   147
Lab Cleanup   147

10. **Configuring Network Health   150**

Exercise 10.1: Installing Active Directory Certificate Services   153
Exercise 10.2: Configuring Certificate Revocation   155
Exercise 10.3: Configuring Certificate Templates   157
Exercise 10.4: Configuring Certificate Enrollment   159
Exercise 10.5: Configuring Network Access Protection (NAP) (optional)   161
Lab Review Questions   164

Lab Challenge: Testing Network
    Access Protection Auto-
    Remediation   165
Lab Cleanup   165

11. Maintaining Windows Server 2008

File Services   167

Exercise 11.1: Installing and
    Configuring Shadow Copies   169
Exercise 11.2: Confirming Shadow
    Copies Functionality   171

Exercise 11.3: Installing and
    Configuring Windows Server
    Backup   173
Exercise 11.4: Installing and
    Configuring Disk Quotas   175
Lab Review Questions   177
Lab Challenge: Creating File
    Screens   178
Lab Cleanup   178

Troubleshooting Lab   179

LAB 1
INTRODUCING WINDOWS SERVER 2008 NETWORKING

This lab contains the following exercises and activities:

Exercise 1.1   Modifying Basic Server Settings

Exercise 1.2   Configuring TCP/IP Settings

Exercise 1.3   Configuring a Second Windows Server 2008 Computer

Exercise 1.4   Configuring a Windows Server 2008 Server Core Computer (optional)

Lab Review   Questions

Lab Challenge   Configuring the Windows Firewall

BEFORE YOU BEGIN

Lab 1 assumes that setup has been completed as specified in the setup document and that your computer has connectivity to other lab computers and the Internet.

For subsequent labs, mandatory exercises require the use of two (2) Windows Server 2008 Enterprise Edition servers. Additionally, optional exercises are provided that involve a server running Windows Server 2008 Server Core and a workstation running Windows Vista Enterprise Edition. You can use multiple physical computers, or you can use Microsoft Virtual PC or Virtual Server to install and run multiple servers on a single machine.

The instructor PC is preconfigured as a domain controller in the lucernepublishing.com domain for demonstration purposes and is named INSTRUCTOR01.

NOTE	*In this lab manual, you will see the characters xx, yy, and zz. These directions assume that you are working on computers configured in pairs and that each computer has a number. One number is odd, and the other number is even. For example, W2K801 is the odd-numbered computer, and W2K802 is the even-numbered computer. When you see xx, substitute the unique number assigned to the odd-numbered computer. When you see yy, substitute the unique number assigned to the even-numbered computer. When you see zz, substitute the number assigned to the computer that you are working at, either odd or even.*

The three Windows Server 2008 server computers will be configured with static IP addresses. For ease of reference, record the static IP addresses of each server that you will be working with in this lab:

INSTRUCTOR01 (Instructor Computer)

IP Address: ___.___.___.___

Subnet Mask: ___.___.___.___

Default Gateway: ___.___.___.___

W2K8*xx*: (For example: W2K801)

IP Address: ___.___.___.___

Subnet Mask: ___.___.___.___

Default Gateway: ___.___.___.___

W2K8*yy*: (For example: W2K802)

IP Address: ___.___.___.___

Subnet Mask: ___.___.___.___

Default Gateway: ___.___.___.___

CORE*xx*: (For example: CORE01)

IP Address: ___.___.___.___

Subnet Mask: ___.___.___.___

Default Gateway: ___.___.___.___

SCENARIO

You are a network support specialist for Lucerne Publishing. Lucerne Publishing has implemented the lucernepublishing.com Active Directory forest as a single-domain environment. You are responsible for preparing several Windows Server 2008 servers to be deployed as file servers, DNS servers, and other infrastructure servers in remote offices. Because these servers were configured with only the default installation options, you have several tasks.

After completing this lab, you will be able to:

- Explore the Windows Server 2008 server interface to become familiar with its administration

- Modify basic settings on a Windows Server 2008 server

- Configure TCP/IP to prepare the Windows Server 2008 computer

- (Optional) Configure a Server Core computer

Estimated lab time: 100 minutes

Exercise 1.1	Modifying Basic Server Settings
Overview	You have just installed a new Windows Server 2008 computer using the default installation settings. You need to modify some basic settings on the server before you can configure it as an infrastructure server.
Outcomes	After completing this exercise, you will know how to: ▲ Log on to a Windows Server 2008 computer ▲ Explore the Initial Configuration Tasks interface ▲ Modify basic settings on a Windows Server 2008 computer
Completion time	10 minutes
Precautions	If the lab instructor has reversed the order of Labs 1 and 2, you may skip this exercise because its steps are encompassed in Lab Exercise 2.2.

1. Press Ctrl+Alt+Delete on the odd-numbered computer, and log on as the default administrator of the local computer. Your username is Administrator. The password is MSPress#1 or the password that your instructor or lab proctor assigns to you. The Initial Configuration Tasks (ICT) window will display automatically.

2. Expand the ICT window to fill the screen if necessary.

Question 1	*What three categories of tasks are listed in the ICT interface?*

Question 2	*What is the current time zone configured for this computer?*

3. Click Set time zone. The Date and Time window will be displayed.

4. Click Change time zone. The Time zone settings window will be displayed.

5. In the Time zone drop-down box, select the appropriate time zone, and click OK. You will return to the Date and Time window.

Question 3	*Why does a shield icon appear next to the Change date and time button?*

6. Click OK to return to the ICT window.

7. Click Enable automatic updating and feedback. The Enable Windows Automated Updating and Feedback window opens. Click Enable Windows automatic updating and feedback (recommended).

8. Click Provide computer name and domain. The System Properties window will be displayed.

Question 4	*What is the current name of your computer?*

9. On the Computer Name tab, click Change. The Computer Name/Domain Changes window is displayed.

10. In the Computer name text box, key **W2K8***xx* for your computer name, where *xx* corresponds to the odd-numbered computer that your instructor or lab proctor has assigned to you. Click OK. A Computer Name/Domain Changes dialog box is displayed, informing you that you must restart your computer to apply these changes. Click OK to acknowledge this dialog box.

11. Click Close to close the System Properties window. You will be prompted to restart your computer to apply the name change. Click Restart Now. Your Windows Server 2008 computer will restart.

Exercise 1.2	Configuring TCP/IP Settings
Overview	Your manager assigned to you the task of preparing a new Windows Server 2008 computer to function as an infrastructure server. To begin, you must configure this computer with static IP address settings.
Outcomes	After completing this exercise, you will know how to: ▲ Configure network settings on a Windows Server 2008 computer
Completion time	15 minutes
Precautions	1. The instructions presume that the lab environment has been configured using the 192.168.1.0/24 Class C address range, with addresses 192.168.1.100–192.168.1.130 reserved for assigning static IP addresses to student computers. If your lab environment uses a different IP addressing scheme, your instructor or lab proctor will provide the appropriate IP addressing values. 2. If the lab instructor has reversed the order of Labs 1 and 2, you may skip this exercise because its steps are encompassed in Lab Exercise 2.2.

1. Press Ctrl+Alt+Delete on the W2K8*xx* computer, and log on as the default administrator of the local computer. Your username will be Administrator. The password will be MSPress#1 or the password that your instructor or lab proctor assigns to you. The Initial Configuration Tasks (ICT) window will be displayed automatically.

2. Place a checkmark next to Do not show this window at logon. Click Close to close the ICT window. The Server Manager window is displayed automatically. Expand the Server Manager window to fill the screen if necessary.

Question 5	What name is assigned to your computer?

3. Click View Network Connections. The Network Connections window is displayed.

NOTE	You can also configure network settings from the ICT screen.

4. Right-click your network connection, and select Properties. The network connection's Properties window will be displayed.

Question 6	What network components are installed on your computer?

5. Click Internet Protocol Version 4 (TCP/IPv4), and select Properties. The Internet Protocol Version 4 (TCP/IPv4) Properties window will be displayed.

Question 7	What IP addressing settings are configured by default?

6. Select the Use the following IP address: radio button. Enter the following IP address information for the odd-numbered computer that you recorded at the beginning of this lab.

   IP Address: for example, 192.168.1.101

   Subnet Mask: for example, 255.255.255.0

   Default Gateway: for example, 192.168.1.1

7. Click OK, and then click Close to save your changes. Close the Network Connections window.

8. Log off of the W2K8*xx* computer.

Exercise 1.3	Configuring a Second Windows Server 2008 Computer
Overview	Your manager assigned to you the task of preparing an additional Windows Server 2008 computer to function as an infrastructure server in one of your branch offices. To begin, you must set up this computer with basic configuration information and static IP address settings.
Outcomes	After completing this exercise, you will know how to: ▲ Log on to a Windows Server 2008 computer ▲ Explore the Initial Configuration Tasks interface ▲ Modify basic settings on a Windows Server 2008 computer ▲ Configure network settings on a Windows Server 2008 computer
Completion time	25 minutes
Precautions	If the lab instructor has reversed the order of Labs 1 and 2, you may skip this exercise because its steps are encompassed in Lab Exercise 2.3.

■ PART A: CONFIGURING BASIC SETTINGS ON THE SECOND WINDOWS SERVER 2008 COMPUTER

1. Press Ctrl+Alt+Delete on the even-numbered computer assigned to you, and log on as the default administrator of the local computer. Your username will be Administrator. The password will be MSPress#1 or the password that your instructor or lab proctor assigns to you. The Initial Configuration Tasks (ICT) window will be displayed automatically. Expand the ICT window to fill the full screen if necessary.

2. Click Set time zone. The Date and Time window will be displayed.

3. Click Change time zone. The Time zone settings window will be displayed.

4. In the Time zone drop-down box, select the appropriate time zone, and click OK. You will return to the Date and Time window.

5. Click OK to return to the ICT window.

6. Click Enable automatic updating and feedback. Click Enable Windows automatic updating and feedback (recommended).

7. Click Provide computer name and domain. The System Properties window will be displayed.

Question 8	*What is the current name of your computer?*

8. On the Computer Name tab, click Change. The Computer Name/Domain Changes window will appear.

9. In the Computer name text box, enter **W2K8**_yy_ for your computer name, where _yy_ corresponds to the even-numbered computer that your instructor or lab proctor has assigned to you. Click OK. A Computer Name/Domain Changes dialog box will be displayed, informing you that you must restart your computer to apply these changes. Click OK to acknowledge this dialog box.

10. Click Close to close the System Properties window. You will be prompted to restart your computer to apply the name change. Click Restart Now. Your Windows Server 2008 computer will restart.

■ PART B: CONFIGURING A STATIC IP ADDRESS ON THE SECOND WINDOWS SERVER 2008 COMPUTER

1. Press Ctrl+Alt+Delete on the W2K8*yy* server, and log on as the default administrator of the local computer. Your username will be Administrator. The password will be MSPress#1 or the password that your instructor or lab proctor assigns to you. The ICT window will be displayed automatically.

2. Place a checkmark next to Do not show this window at logon. Click Close to close the ICT window. The Server Manager screen will be displayed automatically. Expand the Server Manager window to fit the full screen if necessary.

Question 9	*What is the current name of your computer?*

3. Click View Network Connections. The Network Connections window will be displayed.

4. Right-click your network connection, and select Properties. The network connection's Properties window will be displayed.

5. Click Internet Protocol Version 4 (TCP/IPv4), and select Properties. The Internet Protocol Version 4 (TCP/IPv4) Properties window will be displayed.

6. Select the Use the following IP address radio button. Enter the following IP address information for the even-numbered computer that you recorded at the beginning of this lab.

   IP Address: for example, 192.168.1.102

   Subnet Mask: for example, 255.255.255.0

   Default Gateway: for example, 192.168.1.1

7. Click OK, and then click Close to save your changes. Close the Network Connections window.

8. Log off of the W2K8*yy* server.

Exercise 1.4 (optional)	Configuring a Windows Server 2008 Server Core Computer
Overview	Your manager assigned to you the task of preparing an additional Windows Server 2008 computer running Server Core to function as an infrastructure server in one of your branch offices. To begin, you must set up this third Windows Server 2008 computer with basic configuration information and static IP address settings. Because this server is running the Server Core installation option, you must perform most configurations procedures from the command line.
Outcomes	After completing this exercise, you will know how to: ▲ Log on to a Windows Server 2008 Server Core computer ▲ Modify basic settings on a Windows Server 2008 Server Core computer ▲ Configure network settings on a Windows Server 2008 Server Core computer ▲ Enable remote administration exceptions in the Windows Firewall of a Server Core computer
Completion time	20 minutes
Precautions	If the lab instructor has reversed the order of Labs 1 and 2, you may skip this exercise because its steps are encompassed in Lab Exercise 2.4.

■ PART A: CONFIGURING THE SERVER TIME ZONE AND COMPUTER NAME

1. Press Ctrl+Alt+Delete on the third Windows Server 2008 computer assigned to you, and log on as the default administrator of the local computer. Your username will be Administrator. The password will be MSPress#1 or the password that your instructor or lab proctor assigns to you.

Question 10	*What do you see when you log on to a Server Core computer?*

2. Key **timedate.cpl** at the command prompt, and press Enter. The Date and Time window is displayed.

3. Click Change time zone. The Time zone settings window will be displayed.

4. In the Time zone drop-down box, select the appropriate time zone, and click OK. You will return to the Date and Time window. Click OK to return to the command prompt.

5. Key **hostname** at the command prompt, and press Enter.

Question 11	What is the current name of the computer?

6. Key **netdom /?** at the command prompt, and press Enter.

Question 12	What functions can you perform with the netdom command?

7. At the command prompt, key **netdom renamecomputer %computername% /newname:CORExx**, and press Enter.

Question 13	What warning is displayed on the screen?

8. Key **y**, and then press Enter.

Question 14	What message is displayed on the screen?

9. Key **shutdown /r** at the command prompt, and press Enter. A pop-up window informs you that Windows will shut down in less than a minute. Click Close, and allow the computer to restart.

■ PART B: CONFIGURING A STATIC IP ADDRESS.

1. Press Ctrl+Alt+Delete on CORExx, and log on as the default administrator of the local computer. Your username will be Administrator. The password will be MSPress#1 or the password that your instructor or lab proctor assigns to you.

2. Key **ipconfig /all** at the command prompt, and press Enter. Scroll through the ipconfig output to see all presented information.

Question 15	*Is the server receiving its IP configuration via DHCP? How can you tell?*

3. Key **netsh** at the command prompt, and then press Enter. Key **?**, and press Enter.

Question 16	*What are some of the subcommands are available from the netsh menu?*

4. Key **interface**, and then press Enter. Key **?**, and press Enter.

Question 17	*What are some of the subcommands that are available from the interface submenu?*

5. Key **ipv4**, and then press Enter. Key **?**, and press Enter.

Question 18	*What subcommands are available from the ipv4 submenu?*

6. Key **set address name="Local Area Connection" source=static address=<IP Address> mask=<Subnet Mask> gateway=<Default Gateway> gwmetric=1**. Press Enter to assign the appropriate static IP configuration as recorded at the beginning of the lab manual. Key **exit** to return to the command prompt.

7. Key **ipconfig /all**, and press Enter.

Question 19	*Is the computer's IP address now statically assigned?*

8. At the command prompt, key **shutdown /l**, and then press Enter to log off of the CORE*xx* computer.

■ PART C: ENABLING REMOTE ADMINISTRATION OF THE SERVER CORE COMPUTER

1. Press Ctrl+Alt+Delete on the third Windows Server 2008 computer, and log on as the default administrator of the local computer. Your username will be Administrator. The password will be MSPress#1 or the password that your instructor or lab proctor assigns to you.

2. At the command prompt, key **netsh advfirewall set allprofiles settings remotemanagement enable** to allow remote access to the server via the Computer Management MMC, the C$ shares, and so forth, and then press Enter.

3. At the command prompt, key **shutdown /l**, and then press Enter to log off of the computer.

LAB REVIEW QUESTIONS

Completion time	15 minutes

1. In your own words, describe what you learned by completing this lab.

2. Open the Server Manager console on your Windows Server 2008 computer. What selections are available to you in the left pane?

3. Using the Windows Help option, describe any roles and features that are currently installed on this server.

4. Explain in your own words why it is a best practice to configure a server, such as a DNS server, with a static IP address rather than allowing it to obtain an IP address using DHCP.

5. Explore the netsh command menus. Record three commands that you can issue from the command line using netsh, and describe what each command does.

LAB CHALLENGE: CONFIGURING THE WINDOWS FIREWALL

Completion time   15 minutes

Your manager just completed the installation of a new file server that will be used in the lucernepublishing.com domain. You want to configure the Windows Firewall to allow the File & Printer exception on the server.

After completing this exercise, you will know how to:

▲ Configure a Windows Firewall exception on a Windows Server 2008 computer.

Configure the File & Printer Sharing Windows Firewall exception on each Windows Server 2008 computer. Use the Help and Support function from the Start menu to assist you in this procedure. You will use the Windows Firewall Control Panel applet on the W2K8*xx* and/or W2K8*yy* computers and the netsh command-line utility on the CORE*xx* computer.

LAB 2
INSTALLING MICROSOFT WINDOWS SERVER 2008

This lab contains the following exercises and activities:

Exercise 2.1   Installing Windows Server 2008

Exercise 2.2   Configuring Windows Server 2008

Exercise 2.3   Installing and Configuring a Second Windows Server 2008 Computer

Exercise 2.4   Installing and Configuring a Windows Server 2008 Server Core Computer (optional)

Exercise 2.5   Installing and Configuring a Windows Vista Computer (optional)

Lab Review   Questions

Lab Challenge Joining an Active Directory Domain

BEFORE YOU BEGIN

Lab 2 assumes that setup has been completed as specified in the setup document and that your computer has connectivity to other lab computers and the Internet.

For subsequent labs, mandatory exercises require the use of two (2) Windows Server 2008 Enterprise Edition servers. Additionally, optional exercises are provided that involve a server running Windows Server 2008 Server Core and a workstation running Windows Vista Enterprise Edition. You can use multiple physical computers, or you can use Microsoft Virtual PC or Virtual Server to install and run multiple servers on a single machine. This manual assumes you are using multiple virtual machines under Microsoft Virtual PC. In the optional exercises for this lab, Exercises 2.4 and 2.5, you will perform the prerequisite configuration of the Server Core and Vista computers necessary to perform the optional exercises in future lessons.

The instructor PC is preconfigured as a domain controller in the lucernepublishing.com domain for demonstration purposes and is named INSTRUCTOR01.

NOTE	*In this lab manual, you will see the characters xx, yy, and zz. These directions assume that you are working on computers configured in pairs and that each computer has a number. One number is odd, and the other number is even. For example, W2K801 is the odd-numbered computer, and W2K802 is the even-numbered computer. When you see xx, substitute the unique number assigned to the odd-numbered computer. When you see yy, substitute the unique number assigned to the even-numbered computer. When you see zz, substitute the number assigned to the computer that you are working at, either odd or even.*

The four Windows Server 2008 server computers referenced in this lab will each be configured with static IP addresses. For ease of reference, record the static IP addresses of each server that you will be working with in this lab:

INSTRUCTOR01 (Instructor Computer)

IP Address: ___.___.___.___

Subnet Mask: ___.___.___.___

Default Gateway: ___.___.___.___

W2K8*xx*: (For example: W2K801)

IP Address: ___.___.___.___

Subnet Mask: ___.___.___.___

Default Gateway: ___.___.___.___

W2K8*yy*: (For example: W2K802)

IP Address: ___.___.___.___

Subnet Mask: ___.___.___.___

Default Gateway: ___.___.___.___

CORE*xx*: (For example: CORE01)

IP Address: ___.___.___.___

Subnet Mask: ___.___.___.___

Default Gateway: ___.___.___.___

SCENARIO

You are a network support specialist for Lucerne Publishing. Lucerne Publishing has implemented the lucernepublishing.com Active Directory forest as a single-domain environment. After preparing several pre-installed Windows Server 2008 servers to be deployed as file servers, DNS servers, and other infrastructure servers in remote offices, you are informed by IT management that several new offices are about to open that will also require new servers to be installed.

After completing this lab, you will be able to:

- Install and configure the Windows Server 2008 operating system

- (Optional) Install and configure a Server Core computer

- (Optional) Install and configure a Windows Vista workstation

Estimated lab time: 155 minutes

Exercise 2.1	Installing Windows Server 2008
Overview	You have just procured a new machine on which you now need to install the Windows Server 2008 operating system. You have the Windows Server 2008 installation media available.
Outcomes	After completing this exercise, you will know how to: ▲ Install the Windows Server 2008 operating system
Completion time	20 minutes
Precautions	N/A

1. Either insert the Windows Server 2008 media into the appropriate disk drive on the odd-numbered computer, or configure the virtual machine to use an ISO file as indicated by your lab instructor or proctor. Reboot the Windows Server 2008 server or virtual machine. The Install Windows screen appears.

Question 1	*What drop-down boxes are available on the initial installation screen?*

2. Select the appropriate values for the Language to Install, Time and Currency Format, and Keyboard or Input Method drop-down boxes as provided by your instructor or lab proctor. Click Next, and then click Install now.

3. The Select the operating system you want to install screen appears. Select Windows Server 2008 Enterprise (Full Installation), and then click Next.

4. The Please Read the License Terms screen appears. Read the terms of the Windows Server 2008 license agreement, place a checkmark next to I accept the license terms, and then click Next.

5. The Which Type of Installation Do You Want? screen appears.

Question 2	*Why is the Upgrade option disabled?*

6. Click the Custom (advanced) selection. The Where do you want to install Windows? screen appears. Accept the default selection, and click Next.

7. The Installing Windows screen appears. Allow the installation to progress; the computer will reboot multiple times during the process.

8. After the final reboot, you will be prompted to set an initial password for the operating system installation. Click OK. Enter **MSPress#1** as the local Administrator password, and then re-enter the password to confirm.

9. Click the blue arrow to set the initial password, and then click OK.

NOTE	*If you are working with virtualization software, such as Virtual PC, you should now install any software extensions that come with the virtual software to improve the performance of the virtual machine.*

Exercise 2.2	Configuring Windows Server 2008
Overview	You have just installed a new Windows Server 2008 computer using the default installation settings. You need to modify some basic settings on the server before you can configure it as an infrastructure server.
Outcomes	After completing this exercise, you will know how to: ▲ Log on to a Windows Server 2008 computer ▲ Explore the Initial Configuration Tasks interface ▲ Modify basic settings on a Windows Server 2008 computer ▲ Configure network settings on a Windows Server 2008 computer
Completion time	20 minutes
Precautions	The instructions presume that the lab environment has been configured using the 192.168.1.0/24 Class C address range, with addresses 192.168.1.100–192.168.1.130 reserved for assigning static IP addresses to student computers. If your lab environment uses a different IP addressing scheme, your instructor or lab proctor will provide the appropriate IP addressing values.

■ PART A: CONFIGURING BASIC SETTINGS ON A WINDOWS SERVER 2008 COMPUTER

1. Press Ctrl+Alt+Delete on the newly installed computer, and log on as the default administrator of the local computer. Your username is Administrator. The password is MSPress#1 or the password that your instructor or lab proctor assigns to you. The Initial Configuration Tasks (ICT) window will be displayed automatically.

2. Expand the ICT window to fill the screen if necessary.

3. Click Set time zone. The Date and Time window will be displayed.

4. Click Change time zone. The Time zone settings window will be displayed.

5. In the Time zone drop-down box, select the appropriate time zone, and click OK. You will return to the Date and Time window.

6. Click OK to return to the ICT window.

7. Click Enable automatic updating and feedback. The Enable Windows Automated Updating and Feedback window opens. Click Enable Windows automatic updating and feedback (recommended).

8. Click Provide computer name and domain. The System Properties window will be displayed.

9. On the Computer Name tab, click Change. The Computer Name/Domain Changes window is displayed.

10. In the Computer name text box, key **W2K8xx** for your computer name, where *xx* corresponds to the odd-numbered computer that your instructor or lab proctor has assigned to you. Click OK. A Computer Name/Domain Changes dialog box is displayed, informing you that you must restart your computer to apply these changes. Click OK to acknowledge this dialog box.

11. Click Close to close the System Properties window. You will be prompted to restart your computer to apply the name change. Click Restart Now. Your Windows Server 2008 computer will restart.

■ PART B: CONFIGURING TCP/IP SETTINGS ON A WINDOWS SERVER 2008 COMPUTER

1. Press Ctrl+Alt+Delete on the W2K8xx computer, and log on as the default administrator of the local computer. Your username will be Administrator. The password will be MSPress#1 or the password that your instructor or lab proctor assigns to you. The ICT window will be displayed automatically.

2. Place a checkmark next to Do not show this window at logon. Click Close to close the ICT window. The Server Manager window is displayed automatically. Expand the Server Manager window to fill the screen if necessary.

3. Click View Network Connections. The Network Connections window is displayed.

4. Right-click your network connection, and select Properties. The network connection's Properties window will be displayed.

Question 3	*What network components are installed on your computer?*

5. Click Internet Protocol Version 4 (TCP/IPv4), and select Properties. The Internet Protocol Version 4 (TCP/IPv4) Properties window will be displayed.

6. Select the Use the following IP address: radio button. Enter the following IP address information for the instructor computer that you recorded at the beginning of this lab.

IP Address: for example, 192.168.1.101

Subnet Mask: for example, 255.255.255.0

Default Gateway: for example, 192.168.1.1

7. Click OK, and then click Close to save your changes. Close the Network Connections window.

8. Log off of the W2K8xx computer.

Exercise 2.3	Installing and Configuring a Second Windows Server 2008 Computer
Overview	Your manager assigned to you the task of installing and configuring an additional Windows Server 2008 computer to function as an infrastructure server in one of your branch offices. To begin, you must install the operating system on this server, after which you must set up this computer with basic configuration information and static IP address settings.
Outcomes	After completing this exercise, you will know how to: ▲ Log on to a Windows Server 2008 computer ▲ Explore the Initial Configuration Tasks interface ▲ Modify basic settings on a Windows Server 2008 computer ▲ Configure network settings on a Windows Server 2008 computer
Completion time	25 minutes
Precautions	N/A

■ PART A: INSTALLING THE WINDOWS SERVER 2008 OPERATING SYSTEM ON A SECOND COMPUTER

1. Either insert the Windows Server 2008 media into the appropriate disk drive on the even-numbered computer, or configure the virtual machine to use an ISO file as indicated by your lab instructor or proctor. Reboot the Windows Server 2008 server or virtual machine. The Install Windows screen appears.

2. Select the appropriate values for the Language to Install, Time and Currency Format, and Keyboard or Input Method drop-down boxes as provided by your instructor or lab proctor. Click Next, and then click Install now.

3. The Select the operating system you want to install screen appears. Select Windows Server 2008 Enterprise (Full Installation), and then click Next.

4. The Please read the license terms screen appears. Read the terms of the Windows Server 2008 license agreement, place a checkmark next to I accept the license terms, and then click Next.

5. The Which type of installation do you want? screen appears.

6. Click the Custom (advanced) selection. The Where do you want to install Windows? screen appears. Accept the default selection, and click Next.

7. The Installing Windows screen appears. Allow the installation to progress; the computer will reboot multiple times during the process.

8. After the final reboot, you will be prompted to set an initial password for the operating system installation. Click OK. Enter **MSPress#1** as the local Administrator password, and then re-enter the password to confirm.

9. Click the blue arrow to set the initial password, and then click OK.

> **NOTE**
>
> *If you are working with virtualization software, such as Virtual PC, you should now install any software extensions that come with the virtual software to improve the performance of the virtual machine.*

■ PART B: CONFIGURING BASIC SETTINGS ON THE SECOND WINDOWS SERVER 2008 COMPUTER

1. Press Ctrl+Alt+Delete on the newly installed second computer assigned to you, and log on as the default administrator of the local computer. Your username will be Administrator. The password will be MSPress#1 or the password that your instructor or lab proctor assigns to you. The Initial Configuration Tasks (ICT) window will be displayed automatically. Expand the ICT window to fill the full screen if necessary.

2. Click Set time zone. The Date and Time window will be displayed.

3. Click Change time zone. The Time zone settings window will be displayed.

4. In the Time zone drop-down box, select the appropriate time zone, and click OK. You will return to the Date and Time window.

5. Click OK to return to the ICT window.

6. Click Enable automatic updating and feedback. Click Enable Windows automatic updating and feedback (recommended).

7. Click Provide computer name and domain. The System Properties window will be displayed.

Question 4	*What is the current name of your computer?*

8. On the Computer Name tab, click Change. The Computer Name/Domain Changes window will appear.

9. In the Computer name text box, enter **W2K8***yy* for your computer name, where *yy* corresponds to the even-numbered computer that your instructor or lab proctor has assigned to you. Click OK. A Computer Name/Domain Changes dialog box will be displayed, informing you that you must restart your computer to apply these changes. Click OK to acknowledge this dialog box.

10. Click Close to close the System Properties window. You will be prompted to restart your computer to apply the name change. Click Restart Now. Your Windows Server 2008 computer will restart.

■ PART C: CONFIGURING A STATIC IP ADDRESS ON THE SECOND WINDOWS SERVER 2008 COMPUTER

1. Press Ctrl+Alt+Delete on the W2K8*yy* server, and log on as the default administrator of the local computer. Your username will be Administrator. The password will be MSPress#1 or the password that your instructor or lab proctor assigns to you. The Initial Configuration Tasks (ICT) window will be displayed automatically.

2. Place a checkmark next to Do not show this window at logon. Click Close to close the ICT window. The Server Manager screen will be displayed automatically. Expand the Server Manager window to fit the full screen if necessary.

Question 5	*What is the current name of your computer?*

3. Click View Network Connections. The Network Connections window will be displayed.

4. Right-click your network connection, and select Properties. The network connection's Properties window will be displayed.

5. Click Internet Protocol Version 4 (TCP/IPv4), and select Properties. The Internet Protocol Version 4 (TCP/IPv4) Properties window will be displayed.

6. Select the Use the following IP address radio button. Enter the following IP address information for the Read-Only DC that you recorded at the beginning of this lab.

   IP Address: for example, 192.168.1.102

   Subnet Mask: for example, 255.255.255.0

   Default Gateway: for example, 192.168.1.1

7. Click OK, and then click Close to save your changes. Close the Network Connections window.

8. Log off of the W2K8*yy* server.

Exercise 2.4 (optional)	Installing and Configuring a Windows Server 2008 Server Core Computer
Overview	Your manager assigned to you the task of preparing an additional Windows Server 2008 computer running Server Core to function as an infrastructure server in one of your branch offices. To begin, you must install and configure this third Windows Server 2008 computer with basic configuration information and static IP address settings. Because this server is running the Server Core installation option, you must perform most of the configuration from the command line.
Outcomes	After completing this exercise, you will know how to: ▲ Install the Windows Server 2008 Server Core operating system installation option ▲ Log on to a Windows Server 2008 Server Core computer ▲ Modify basic settings on a Windows Server 2008 Server Core computer ▲ Configure network settings on a Windows Server 2008 Server Core computer ▲ Enable remote administration exceptions in the Windows Firewall of a Server Core computer
Completion time	30 minutes
Precautions	N/A

■ PART A: INSTALLING WINDOWS SERVER 2008 SERVER CORE

1. Either insert the Windows Server 2008 media into the appropriate disk drive, or configure the virtual machine to use an ISO file as indicated by your lab

instructor or proctor. Reboot the Windows Server 2008 server or virtual machine. The Install Windows screen appears.

2. Select the appropriate values for the Language to Install, Time and Currency Format, and Keyboard or Input Method drop-down boxes as provided by your instructor or lab proctor. Click Next, and then click Install now.

3. The Select the operating system you want to install screen appears. Select Windows Server 2008 Enterprise (Server Core Installation), and then click Next.

4. The Please read the license terms screen appears. Read the terms of the Windows Server 2008 license agreement, place a checkmark next to I accept the license terms, and then click Next.

5. The Which type of installation do you want? screen appears.

6. Click the Custom (advanced) selection. The Where do you want to install Windows? screen appears. Accept the default selection, and click Next.

7. The Installing Windows screen appears. Allow the installation to progress; the computer will reboot multiple times during the process.

8. After the final reboot, you will be presented with an "Other User" login prompt. Log on as Administrator with a blank password, after which you will be prompted to set an initial password for the operating system installation. Click OK. Enter **MSPress#1** as the new local Administrator password, and then re-enter the password to confirm.

9. Click the blue arrow to set the initial password, and then click OK.

> **NOTE**
>
> *If you are working with virtualization software, such as Virtual PC, you should now install any software extensions that come with the virtual software to improve the performance of the virtual machine.*

■ PART B: CONFIGURING THE SERVER TIME ZONE AND COMPUTER NAME.

1. Press Ctrl+Alt+Delete on the third Windows Server 2008 computer assigned to you, and log on as the default administrator of the local computer. Your username will be Administrator. The password will be MSPress#1 or the password that your instructor or lab proctor assigns to you.

Question 6	*What do you see when you log on to a Server Core computer?*

2. Key **timedate.cpl** at the command prompt, and press Enter. The Date and Time window is displayed.

3. Click Change time zone. The Time zone settings window will be displayed.

4. In the Time zone drop-down box, select the appropriate time zone, and click OK. You will return to the Date and Time window. Click OK to return to the command prompt.

5. Key **hostname** at the command prompt, and press Enter.

6. Key **netdom /?**, at the command prompt, and press Enter.

7. At the command prompt, key **netdom renamecomputer %computername% /newname:CORE*xx***, and press Enter.

8. Key **y**, and then press Enter.

9. Key **shutdown /r** at the command prompt, and press Enter. A pop-up window informs you that Windows will shut down in less than a minute. Click Close, and allow the computer to restart.

■ PART C: CONFIGURING A STATIC IP ADDRESS.

1. Press Ctrl+Alt+Delete on CORE*xx*, and log on as the default administrator of the local computer. Your username will be Administrator. The password will be MSPress#1 or the password that your instructor or lab proctor assigns to you.

2. Key **ipconfig /all** at the command prompt, and press Enter.

3. Key **netsh**, and then press Enter. Key **?**, and press Enter.

4. Key **interface**, and then press Enter. Key **?**, and press Enter.

5. Key **ipv4**, and then press Enter. Key **?**, and press Enter.

6. Key **set address name="Local Area Connection" source=static address=<IP Address> mask=<Subnet Mask> gateway=<Default Gateway> gwmetric=1**. Press Enter to assign the appropriate static IP configuration as recorded at the beginning of Lab 2. Key **exit** to return to the command prompt.

7. Key **ipconfig /all**, and press Enter.

8. Log off of the CORExx computer.

■ **PART D: ENABLING REMOTE ADMINISTRATION OF THE SERVER CORE COMPUTER**

1. Press Ctrl+Alt+Delete on CORExx, and log on as the default administrator of the local computer. Your username will be Administrator. The password will be MSPress#1 or the password that your instructor or lab proctor assigns to you.

2. At the command prompt, key **netsh advfirewall set allprofiles settings remotemanagement enable** to allow remote access to the server via the Computer Management MMC, the C$ shares, and so forth, and then press Enter.

3. At the command prompt, key **shutdown /l**, and then press Enter to log off of the computer.

Exercise 2.5 (optional)	Installing and Configuring a Windows Vista Computer
Overview	Your manager assigned to you the task of preparing Windows Vista workstations to be deployed to your branch offices. You must install and configure the Windows Vista operating system to create a consistent image for use in large-scale workstation deployments.
Outcomes	After completing this exercise, you will know how to: ▲ Install the Windows Vista operating system ▲ Log on to a Windows Vista computer ▲ Modify basic settings on a Windows Vista computer ▲ Configure network settings on a Windows Vista computer
Completion time	30 minutes
Precautions	N/A

1. Either insert the Windows Vista Ultimate media into the appropriate disk drive, or configure the virtual machine to use an ISO file as indicated by your lab instructor or proctor. Reboot the Windows Vista workstation or virtual machine. The Install Windows screen appears.

2. Select the appropriate values for the Language to Install, Time and Currency Format, and Keyboard or Input Method drop-down boxes as provided by your instructor or lab proctor. Click Next, and then click Install now.

3.   The Type your product key for activation screen appears. Enter a legitimate Windows Vista product key, and then click Next.

4.   The Please read the license terms screen appears. Read the terms of the Windows Server 2008 license agreement, place a checkmark next to I accept the license terms, and then click Next.

5.   The Which type of installation do you want? screen appears.

6.   Click the Custom (advanced) selection. The Where do you want to install Windows? screen appears. Accept the default selection, and click Next.

7.   The Installing Windows screen appears. Allow the installation to progress; the computer will reboot multiple times during the process.

8.   After the final installation reboot, the Choose a user name and picture screen will appear. In the Type a user name field, enter **STUDENTxx**, where *xx* corresponds to the student number that was assigned by your instructor or lab proctor. In the Type a password field and the Retype your password field, enter **MSPress#1**. In the Type a password hint field, enter **"70-642 Lab Default"**. Click Next.

9.   The Type a computer name and choose a desktop background screen appears. Enter **VISTAxx** as the computer name, and then click Next.

10.   The Help protect windows automatically screen appears. Click Use recommended settings.

11.   The Review your time and date settings screen appears. Enter the appropriate time zone and the current time. Click Next and then Start. If you are prompted for a network location, select Work.

12.   Log off of the VISTAxx computer.

> **NOTE**
> *If you are working with virtualization software, such as Virtual PC, you should now install any software extensions that come with the virtual software to improve the performance of the virtual machine.*

LAB REVIEW QUESTIONS

Completion time	15 minutes

1.   In your own words, describe what you learned by completing this lab.

2. What is the difference between a Full Installation of Windows Server 2008 and installing Windows Server 2008 Server Core?

3. Explore the reg.exe Windows Server 2008 command-line help by keying **reg /?**. Record three commands that you can issue from the command line using the reg utility, and describe what each command does:

LAB CHALLENGE: JOINING AN ACTIVE DIRECTORY DOMAIN

Completion time	15 minutes

You have completed the installation of several Windows Server 2008 and Windows Vista computers on your network. To test several configuration items that are dependent on Active Directory, you wish to join these computers to the lucernepublishing.com Active Directory domain that is hosted on the INSTRUCTOR01 Windows Server 2008 computer.

After completing this exercise, you will know how to:

▲ Join an Active Directory domain

Join each computer in this lab to the lucernepublishing.com Active Directory domain that is hosted on the INSTRUCTOR01 Windows Server 2008 computer. Either use LP\Administrator as the domain credentials to join each computer to the domain with a password of MSPress#1, or use the credentials provided by your instructor or lab proctor.

NOTE	*You will need to configure DNS on each computer to point to INSTRUCTOR01 as its preferred DNS server.*

When you are finished, drop each computer back into a workgroup configuration, and reverse any changes that you made to each computer's network configuration to allow the computer to join the Active Directory domain.

LAB 3
CONFIGURING AND MANAGING THE DHCP SERVER ROLE

This lab contains the following exercises and activities:

Exercise 3.1   Installing the DHCP Server Role

Exercise 3.2   Confirming DHCP Server Functionality

Exercise 3.3   Managing the DHCP Server Role

Exercise 3.4   Installing and Configuring the DHCP Server Role on Server Core (optional)

Lab Review   Questions

Lab Challenge   Authorizing a DHCP Server in Active Directory

Lab Cleanup

BEFORE YOU BEGIN

Lab 3 assumes that setup has been completed as specified in the setup document and that your computer has connectivity to other lab computers and the Internet. The required exercises in Lab 3 also assume that you have completed the required exercises in Lab 2; Exercise 3.4 assumes that you have completed Exercise 2.4 in Lab 2.

The instructor PC is preconfigured as a domain controller in the lucernepublishing.com domain for demonstration purposes and is named INSTRUCTOR01.

In a multi-student classroom, the instructor should also assign a separate DHCP scope to each student or student pairing so that there are no overlapping DHCP scopes in the room. In a Virtual PC environment, this can also be accomplished by configuring the student VMs on separate virtual networks for the duration of Lab 3.

> **NOTE**
>
> *If a DHCP scope is running on the INSTRUCTOR computer or on a hardware-based device such as a classroom router, this must be disabled prior to performing these steps. Since students will install their own DHCP servers, the classroom subnet must be isolated from the rest of the school. In addition, since multiple DHCP servers will be installed on the classroom subnet, be aware that the client connects to the first DHCP server that responds. Therefore, each PC may not connect to the DHCP server that might be expected.*

> **NOTE**
>
> *In this lab manual, you will see the characters xx, yy, and zz. These directions assume that you are working on computers configured in pairs and that each computer has a number. One number is odd, and the other number is even. For example, W2K801 is the odd-numbered computer, and W2K802 is the even-numbered computer. When you see xx, substitute the unique number assigned to the odd-numbered computer. When you see yy, substitute the unique number assigned to the even-numbered computer. When you see zz, substitute the number assigned to the computer that you are working at, either odd or even.*

The four Windows Server 2008 server computers referenced in this lab will each be configured with static IP addresses. For ease of reference, record the static IP addresses of each server that you will be working with in this lab:

INSTRUCTOR01 (Instructor Computer)

IP Address: ___.___.___.___

Subnet Mask: ___.___.___.___

Default Gateway: ___.___.___.___

W2K8*xx*: (For example: W2K801)

IP Address: ___.___.___.___

Subnet Mask: ___.___.___.___

Default Gateway: ___.___.___.___

W2K8*yy*: (For example: W2K802)

IP Address: ___.___.___.___

Subnet Mask: ___.___.___.___

Default Gateway: ___.___.___.___

CORExx: (For example: CORE01)

IP Address: ___.___.___.___

Subnet Mask: ___.___.___.___

Default Gateway: ___.___.___.___

SCENARIO

You are a network administrator for Litware, Inc. Recently, Contoso, Ltd. acquired Litware, Inc. As a result, Litware, Inc. is expanding its network. In the past, Litware, Inc. utilized Automatic Private IP Addressing (APIPA). Because of the increase in the number of clients (which motivated Contoso to acquire Litware, Inc.) and the fact that network administrators installed a router to allow users Internet access, you have been asked to plan and install a dynamic addressing system using Dynamic Host Configuration Protocol (DHCP). You and a partner must work together to install the DHCP Server service and configure it to assign the necessary configuration parameters.

After completing this lab, you will be able to:

- Install and configure the DHCP Server role

- Manage the DHCP Server role

- (Optional) Install and configure the DHCP Server role on a Server Core computer

Estimated lab time: 115 minutes

Exercise 3.1	Installing the DHCP Server Role
Overview	You have just procured a new server to act as a DHCP server on your network.
Outcomes	After completing this exercise, you will know how to: ▲ Install the DHCP Server role ▲ Configure a DHCP scope
Completion time	20 minutes
Precautions	N/A

1. Press Ctrl+Alt+Delete on the W2K8xx Windows Server 2008 computer assigned to you, and log on as the default administrator of the local computer. Your username will be Administrator. The password will be MSPress#1 or the password that your instructor or lab proctor assigns to you.

2. If the Initial Configuration Tasks (ICT) screen window opens automatically, place a checkmark next to Do not show this window at logon, and click Close.

3. If the Server Manager window does not appear automatically, click the Start button, and then click Server Manager.

Question 1	What is the name of the computer you are working from?

4. In the left-hand pane of Server Manager, double-click Roles.

5. Click Add Roles. Click Next to bypass/dismiss the initial Welcome screen.

6. The Select Server Roles screen appears. Place a checkmark next to DHCP Server, and then click Next.

7. The Introduction to DHCP Server screen appears. Click Next.

8. If the Select Network Bindings screen appears, accept the default selection, and click Next. The Specify IPv4 DNS Server Settings screen appears. Leave these settings blank (you will configure them in a later exercise), and click Next

9. The Specify IPv4 WINS Server Settings screen appears. Confirm that the WINS is not required for applications on this network radio button is selected, and click Next.

10. The Add or Edit DHCP Scopes screen appears. Click Add.

11. The Add Scope screen appears. Enter the following information, and click OK.

- Scope Name: **70-642 Lab 3 Exercise 3-1 Scope**

- Starting IP Address: The starting IP address that has been assigned by your instructor or lab proctor

- Ending IP Address: The ending IP address that has been assigned by your instructor or lab proctor

- Subnet Mask: The subnet mask that has been assigned by your instructor or lab proctor

- Default Gateway: The default gateway that has been assigned by your instructor or lab proctor

- Subnet Type: Wired

Question 2	What is the default lease duration of a Wired subnet type?

12. Click Next. The Configure DHCPv6 Stateless Mode screen appears.

13. Click Next twice, and then click Install. Click Close.

14. You will be returned to the Server Manager console. Under the Roles header in the Roles Summary section, click the DHCP Server hyperlink.

15. The DHCP Server window screen appears. Scroll to the Resources and Support section.

Question 3	What are three recommendations listed in Server Manager for managing the DHCP Server role?

16. Log off of the W2K8*xx* computer.

Exercise 3.2	Confirming DHCP Server Functionality
Overview	Now that you have installed and configured a DHCP server, you must confirm that DHCP clients on your network are able to receive IP address configuration from the server.
Outcomes	After completing this exercise, you will know how to: ▲ Configure Windows Server 2008 dynamic IP addressing ▲ Confirm DHCP server functionality
Completion time	10 minutes
Precautions	These steps should be performed on the even-numbered W2K8yy computer.

1. Press Ctrl+Alt+Delete on the W2K8*yy* Windows Server 2008 computer assigned to you, and log on as the default administrator of the local computer. Your username will be Administrator. The password will be MSPress#1 or the password that your instructor or lab proctor assigns to you.

2. If the Initial Configuration Tasks (ICT) screen window opens automatically, place a checkmark next to Do not show this window at logon, and click Close.

3. If the Server Manager window does not appear automatically, click the Start button, and then click Server Manager.

Question 4	What is the name of the computer you are working from?

4. Click View Network Connections. The Network Connections window is displayed.

5. Right-click your network connection, and select Properties. The network connection's Properties window will be displayed.

6. Click Select Internet Protocol Version 4 (TCP/IPv4), and select click Properties. The Internet Protocol Version 4 (TCP/IPv4) Properties window will be displayed.

Question 5	What IP addressing settings are currently configured?

7. Select the Obtain an IP address automatically radio button.

8. Click OK, and then click Close two times to save your changes. Close the Network Connections window.

9. Click Start, key **cmd**, and press Enter.

10. At the command prompt, key **ipconfig /renew**.

11. At the command prompt, key **ipconfig /all**.

Question 6	Is the computer currently configured for DHCP? How can you tell?

Question 7	What is the IP address of the DHCP server from which W2K8yy has obtained its IP address?

Question 8	If the answer to #7 was not the IP address of the W2K8xx computer, why might this have happened?

12. At the command prompt, key **exit**, and press Enter to close the command prompt window.

13. Log off of the W2K8*yy* computer.

Exercise 3.3	Managing the DHCP Server Role
Overview	Having configured the basics of a Windows Server 2008 DHCP server, you will now perform management and maintenance tasks on the server prior to deploying it into a production environment. You will verify any changes in functionality using the W2K8*xx* server that is currently configured to obtain its IP address via DHCP.
Outcomes	After completing this exercise, you will know how to: ▲ Configure DHCP options ▲ Configure DHCP reservations ▲ Back up and restore DHCP ▲ View APIPA IP addresses ▲ Deactivate a DHCP scope
Completion time	25 minutes
Precautions	Each part of this exercise will be performed on either the odd-numbered W2K8*xx* computer or the even-numbered W2K8*yy* computer. The exercise instructions will indicate on which computer each part is to be performed.

■ PART A: CONFIGURING DHCP OPTIONS

1. Log on to the W2K8*xx* server. Click Start→Administrative Tools→DHCP. Expand the DHCP console to full screen if necessary.

2. Expand the W2K8*xx* node, followed by IPv4, followed by Scope [[<address>] 70-642 Lab 3 Exercise 3-1 Scope].

Question 9	*What nodes appear underneath the DHCP scope that you created in Exercise 3-1?*

3. Right-click Scope Options, and click Configure Options….

4. Place a checkmark next to 006 DNS Servers. In the Server name: text box, enter **w2k8xx**, and click Resolve.

Question 10	*What appears in the IP address text box?*

5.   Click Add, and then click OK.

6.   Log off of the odd-numbered computer.

■ PART B: CONFIRMING THE ADDITION OF THE DHCP OPTION

1.   Log on to the W2K8*yy* computer. Open a command prompt, key **ipconfig /renew**, and press Enter.

2.   Key **ipconfig /all**, and press Enter.

Question 11	*What value is configured in the DNS Servers: line?*

3.   Record the Physical address of the even-numbered computer for use in the next Part C.

4.   Log off of the even-numbered computer.

■ PART C: CONFIGURING A DHCP RESERVATION

1.   Log on to the odd-numbered computer. Click Start→Administrative Tools→DHCP.

2.   Expand the W2K8*xx* node, followed by IPv4, followed by Scope [<address>]70-642 Lab 3 Exercise 3-1 Scope].

3.   Click Reservations. Right-click Reservations, and select New Reservation….

4.   In the Reservation Name text box, enter **W2K8*yy***.

5.   In the IP Address: field, enter an available IP address within the scope that you defined at the start of Lab 3.

6.   In the MAC address: field, enter the physical address of the even-numbered computer as indicated in the ipconfig /all output from the even-numbered computer.

7.   Click Add, and then Close.

8. Expand the Reservations node. Right-click the reservation you just created, and click Configure Options….

9. Place a checkmark next to 006 DNS Servers. Enter the IP address that you configured for the DHCP reservation you just created.

10. Click Add, and then click OK.

11. Close the DHCP MMC, and log off of the W2K8*xx* computer.

■ PART D: CONFIRMING THE DHCP RESERVATION

1. Log on to the W2K8*yy* computer. Open a command prompt, key **ipconfig /renew**, and press Enter.

2. At the command prompt, key **ipconfig /all**, and press Enter.

Question 12	What value is configured in the DNS Servers: line?

3. Log off of the even-numbered computer.

■ PART E: BACKING UP A DHCP SERVER

1. Log on to the W2K8*xx* computer. Click Start→Administrative Tools→DHCP.

2. Right-click the W2K8*xx* node, and click Backup…. The Browse for Folder screen appears.

Question 13	What is the default location for DHCP server backups?

3. Browse to the C:\ top-level folder. Click Make New Folder. Key **backup**, and press Enter to create the C:\backup folder. Select the C:\backup folder, and then click OK.

4. To simulate a failure of the DHCP server, right-click the scope that you created in Exercise 3-1, and click Delete. Click Yes twice to confirm.

5. Log off of the odd-numbered computer.

■ PART F: SIMULATING A DHCP FAILURE ON THE CLIENT

1. Reboot the W2K8*yy* computer to simulate the client booting during a failure of the DHCP server.

2. Open a command prompt window. Key **ipconfig**, and press Enter.

Question 14	*What IP address is configured on the W2K8yy computer?*

3. Log off of the even-numbered computer.

■ PART G: RESTORING THE DHCP DATABASE

1. Log on to the W2K8*xx* computer. Click Start→Administrative Tools→DHCP.

2. Right-click the W2K8*xx* node, and click Restore…. The Browse for Folder screen appears.

3. Select the C:\backup folder, and then click OK. Click Yes when prompted to stop and restart the DHCP server service.

NOTE	*If a red down-arrow appears, click F5 to refresh your view until the red arrow changes to green.*

4. Log off of the odd-numbered computer.

■ PART H: CONFIRMING THE RESTORATION ON THE CLIENT

1. Log on to the W2K8*yy* computer. Open a command prompt.

2. Key **ipconfig /renew**, and then press Enter.

Question 15	*What appears in the IP address text box?*

3. Log off of the even-numbered computer.

■ PART I: DEACTIVATING THE DHCP SCOPE

1. Log on to the W2K8*xx* computer. Click Start→Administrative Tools→DHCP.

2. Select the DHCP scope; right-click the scope, and click Deactivate. Click Yes to confirm.

3. Log off of the W2K8xx computer.

Exercise 3.4 (optional)	Installing and Configuring the DHCP Server Role on Server Core
Overview	To increase the security of servers deployed in several remote offices, you have prepared servers running the Windows Server 2008 Server Core installation option to provide infrastructure services to these offices. You must now prepare one of these servers to function as a DHCP server.
Outcomes	After completing this exercise, you will know how to: ▲ Install the DHCP Server role on Server Core ▲ Create a DHCP scope on Server Core ▲ Configure DHCP options on Server Core
Completion time	30 minutes
Precautions	This exercise will be performed on the *CORExx* Server Core computer that you installed in Exercise 2.4 in Lab 2.

■ PART A: INSTALLING AND CONFIGURING THE DHCP SERVER ROLE ON SERVER CORE

1. Press Ctrl+Alt+Delete on the CORE*xx* Windows Server 2008 Server Core computer assigned to you, and log on as the default administrator of the local computer. Your username will be Administrator. The password will be MSPress#1 or the password that your instructor or lab proctor assigns to you.

2. From the command prompt window, key **start /w ocsetup DHCPServerCore**, and then press Enter.

3. At the command prompt, key **sc config dhcpserver start= auto**, and press Enter.

> **NOTE**
>
> *Be sure to include the space between "=" and "auto" or else the command will fail.*

4. At the command prompt, key **net start dhcpserver**, and press Enter.

5. At the command prompt, key **netsh**, and press Enter. Key **dhcp server**, and press Enter.

6. To create the scope, key **add scope <Scope Address> <Scope Subnet Mask> ServerCoreScope**, and press Enter. For example, key **add scope 192.168.100.0 255.255.255.0 ServerCoreScope**, and press Enter.

7. Key **exit**, and then press Enter.

8. At the command prompt, key **Shutdown /l**, and then press Enter to log off of the CORE*xx* computer.

■ PART B: CONFIRMING DHCP FUNCTIONALITY

1. Log on to the W2K8*yy* computer. Open a command prompt, key **ipconfig /renew**, and then press Enter.

> **NOTE**
>
> *If you receive an error message, wait a few minutes and try again.*

2. Key **ipconfig /all**, and then press Enter.

> **Question 16**
>
> *From which DHCP server are you receiving an IP address?*

LAB REVIEW QUESTIONS

Completion time	15 minutes

1. In your own words, describe what you learned by completing this lab.

2. You have installed the DHCP Server service on a computer running Windows Server 2008. You configure and activate a 10.0.0.0/24 scope; however, clients still are receiving a 169.254.*x*.*x* IP address. What should you do?

3. You have configured a DHCP scope with an address range of 192.168.0.1 through 192.168.0.254. You have several servers and printers that use the IP address range of 192.168.0.1 through 192.168.0.20. With the least amount of administrative effort, how can you prevent duplicate IP addressing?

4. You currently are using a DHCP server on your network. It assigns a default gateway scope option to clients. You use a router with a different IP address to replace a router on your network. The new router allows clients to connect to the Internet; however, clients cannot connect to the Internet using the new router. What should you do?

LAB CHALLENGE: AUTHORIZING A DHCP SERVER IN ACTIVE DIRECTORY

Completion time	15 minutes

You have completed the installation of the DHCP Server role on multiple Windows Server 2008 computers. To test DHCP's interoperability with Active Directory, you wish to join one of the DHCP servers to the lucernepublishing.com Active Directory domain that is hosted on the INSTRUCTOR01 Windows Server 2008 computer and then authorize the DHCP server within Active Directory.

After completing this exercise, you will know how to:

▲ Join an Active Directory domain

▲ Authorize a DHCP server in Active Directory

Precautions: If you do not complete the Lab Challenge exercise, you must still complete the Post-Lab Cleanup steps prior to continuing on to Lab 4.

Join each computer in this lab to the lucernepublishing.com Active Directory domain that is hosted on the INSTRUCTOR01 Windows Server 2008 computer; use LP\Administrator as the domain credentials to join each computer to the domain with a password of MSPress#1, or else use the credentials provided by your instructor or lab proctor.

NOTE	*You will need to configure DNS on each computer to point to INSTRUCTOR01 as its preferred DNS server.*

Once the DHCP server has joined the Active Directory domain, use the DHCP MMC snap-in to authorize the DHCP server within Active Directory. Check the Event Viewer on the DHCP server to confirm that the server has been successfully authorized.

LAB CLEANUP

Completion time	15 minutes

You have completed testing of the DHCP server role, and now need to reset your Windows Server 2008 computers to their original state prior to performing testing of additional infrastructure services that you are planning to deploy to your production network.

After completing this exercise, you will know how to:

▲ Remove the DHCP Server role

PART A: REMOVING THE DHCP SERVER ROLE FROM W2K8*XX*

1. Log on to the W2K8*xx* server. If the Server Manager console does not appear automatically, click the Start button, and then click Server Manager.

2. In the left-hand pane of Server Manager, click Roles. In the right-hand pane, click Remove Roles. Click Next

3. The Remove Server Roles screen appears. Remove the checkmark next to DHCP Server, and then click Next.

4. Click Remove, and then click Close when the removal has completed.

5. When prompted, reboot the W2K8*xx* computer.

6. Log on to the W2K8*xx* server after it reboots. The Server Manager console will reappear automatically. Click Finish when prompted.

7. Log off of the W2K8*xx* server.

PART B: CONFIGURING W2K8*YY* WITH A STATIC IP ADDRESS

Using the IP addresses recorded at the beginning of this lab as a reference, reconfigure the even-numbered W2K8*yy* server with a static IP address, subnet mask, and default gateway.

PART C: REMOVING THE DHCP SERVER ROLE FROM CORE*XX*

1. Log on to the CORE*xx* server. At the command prompt, key **start /w ocsetup DHCPServerCore /uninstall**, and press Enter.

2.   When prompted, click Yes to restart the server.

PART D: LAB CHALLENGE CLEANUP

If you completed Lab Challenge 3.1, perform the following cleanup tasks:

- Reverse any changes that you made to the IP configuration of any lab computers, including the preferred or alternate IP address settings.

- Any lab computers that you added into the lucernepublishing.com domain should be switched to a workgroup configuration.

LAB 4
CONFIGURING AND MANAGING THE DNS SERVER ROLE

This lab contains the following exercises and activities:

Exercise 4.1   Installing the DNS Server Role

Exercise 4.2   Configuring a Secondary Zone and Zone Transfers

Exercise 4.3   Configuring Reverse Lookup Zones and Confirming DNS Functionality

Exercise 4.4   Installing and Configuring the DNS Server Role on Server Core (optional)

Lab Review   Questions

Lab Challenge   Configuring DNS Forwarders

Lab Cleanup

BEFORE YOU BEGIN

Lab 4 assumes that setup has been completed as specified in the setup document and that your computer has connectivity to other lab computers and the Internet. The required exercises in Lab 4 also assume that you have completed the exercises in Lab 2; Exercise 4.5 assumes that you have completed Exercise 2.4 in Lab 2.

The instructor PC is preconfigured as a domain controller in the lucernepublishing.com domain for demonstration purposes and is named INSTRUCTOR01.

> **NOTE**
>
> *In this lab manual, you will see the characters xx, yy, and zz. These directions assume that you are working on computers configured in pairs and that each computer has a number. One number is odd, and the other number is even. For example, W2K801 is the odd-numbered computer, and W2K802 is the even-numbered computer. When you see xx, substitute the unique number assigned to the odd-numbered computer. When you see yy, substitute the unique number assigned to the even-numbered computer. When you see zz, substitute the number assigned to the computer that you are working at, either odd or even.*

The four Windows Server 2008 server computers referenced in this lab will each be configured with static IP addresses. For ease of reference, record the static IP addresses of each server that you will be working with in this lab:

INSTRUCTOR01 (Instructor Computer)

IP Address: ___.___.___.___

Subnet Mask: ___.___.___.___

Default Gateway: ___.___.___.___

W2K8xx: (For example: W2K801)

IP Address: ___.___.___.___

Subnet Mask: ___.___.___.___

Default Gateway: ___.___.___.___

W2K8yy: (For example: W2K802)

IP Address: ___.___.___.___

Subnet Mask: ___.___.___.___

Default Gateway: ___.___.___.___

CORExx: (For example: CORE01)

IP Address: ___.___.___.___

Subnet Mask: ___.___.___.___

Default Gateway: ___.___.___.___

You will also need two test IP addresses in the same IP subnet for use in a later exercise. Record these IP addresses here for reference:

TEST*xx*: (For example: TEST01)

IP Address: ___.___.___.___

TEST*yy*: (For example: TEST02)

IP Address: ___.___.___.___

SCENARIO

You are a network administrator for Contoso, Ltd. Recently, Lucerne Publishing has entered into a joint venture with another company, Adatum. As a result, both organizations now have a requirement to be able to resolve the names of servers hosting resources in each organization. You have been asked to plan and install the Domain Name System (DNS) service to provide name resolution for users in both networks. You will need to install the DNS Server service and configure it to assign the necessary configuration parameters.

After completing this lab, you will be able to:

■ Install the DNS Server Role

■ Configure a secondary zone and zone transfers

■ Configure reverse lookup zones and confirming DNS functionality

■ (Optional) Install and configureg the DNS Server Role on Server Core

Estimated lab time:145 minutes

Exercise 4.1	Installing the DNS Server Role
Overview	You have just procured a new server to act as a DNS server on your network.
Outcomes	After completing this exercise, you will know how to: ▲ Install the DNS Server role on Windows Server 2008 ▲ Create primary DNS zones ▲ Create DNS host (A) records
Completion time	20 minutes
Precautions	This exercise will be performed on both the odd-numbered W2K8*xx* computer and the even-numbered W2K8*yy* computer.

■ PART A: INSTALLING THE DNS SERVER ROLE ON THE ODD-NUMBERED COMPUTER

1. Press Ctrl+Alt+Delete on the W2K8*xx* Windows Server 2008 computer assigned to you, and log on as the default administrator of the local computer. Your username will be Administrator. The password will be MSPress#1 or the password that your instructor or lab proctor assigns to you.

2. If the Initial Configuration Tasks (ICT) screen window opens automatically, place a checkmark next to Do not show this window at logon, and click Close.

3. If the Server Manager window does not appear automatically, click the Start button, and then click Server Manager.

Question 1	*What is the name of the computer from which you are working?*

4. In the left-hand pane of Server Manager, double-click Roles.

5. Click Add Roles. Click Next to dismiss the initial Welcome screen.

6. The Select Server Roles screen appears. Place a checkmark next to DNS Server, and then click Next.

7. The Introduction to DNS Server screen appears. Click Next, and then click Install.

8. Click Close when the installation completes.

9. Log off of the odd-numbered computer.

■ PART B: INSTALLING THE DNS SERVER ROLE ON THE EVEN-NUMBERED COMPUTER

1. Press Ctrl+Alt+Delete on the W2K8*yy* Windows Server 2008 computer assigned to you, and log on as the default administrator of the local computer. Your username will be Administrator. The password will be MSPress#1 or the password that your instructor or lab proctor assigns to you.

2. If the ICT screen window opens automatically, place a checkmark next to Do not show this window at logon, and click Close.

3. If the Server Manager window does not appear automatically, click the Start button, and then click Server Manager.

Question 2	What is the name of the computer from which you are working?

4. In the left-hand pane of Server Manager, double-click Roles.

5. Click Add Roles. Click Next to dismiss the initial Welcome screen.

6. The Select Server Roles screen appears. Place a checkmark next to DNS Server, and then click Next.

7. The Introduction to DNS Server screen appears. Click Next, and then click Install.

8. Click Close when the installation completes.

9. Log off of the even-numbered computer.

■ PART C: CONFIGURING A PRIMARY ZONE FOR CONTOSO.COM ON THE ODD-NUMBERRED COMPUTER

NOTE	Be sure to complete these steps on the odd-numbered W2K8xx computer only!

1. Log on to the odd-numbered W2K8*xx* computer. Click Start→Administrative Tools→DNS. Expand the DNS MMC to full screen if necessary.

2. Navigate to W2K8*xx*→Forward Lookup Zones.

Question 3	What forward lookup zones are currently configured on the W2K8xx computer?

3. Right-click Forward Lookup Zones, and click New Zone.... Click Next. The Zone Type screen appears.

Question 4	*What types of zones can you configure from this screen?*

4. Ensure that the Primary zone radio button is selected, and then click Next.

5. The Zone Name screen appears. In the Zone name: text box, key **contoso.com**. Click Next.

6. The Zone File screen appears. Accept the default selection, and click Next.

Question 5	*What is the default selection on the Zone File screen?*

7. The Dynamic Update screen appears. Accept the default selection of "Do not allow dynamic updates," and click Next.

Question 6	*Why is the "allow only secure dynamic updates" option greyed out?*

8. Click Finish. Confirm that contoso.com appears in the list of Forward Lookup Zones configured on W2K8*xx*.

9. Select the contoso.com forward lookup zone.

Question 7	*What records are configured for the contoso.com zone?*

10. Right-click contoso.com, and click New Host (A or AAAA)….

11. The New Host screen appears. In the Name (uses parent domain name if blank): text box, enter **W2K8*xx***. In the IP address: text box, enter the IP address of the W2K8*xx* server.

12. Click Add Host. Click OK, and then click Done to confirm. Confirm that an A record has been added for W2K8*xx*.

13. If the Server Manager console is not open already, click Start➔Server Manager. Click View Network Connections.

14. Right-click Local Area Connection, and click Properties. Double-click Internet Protocol Version 4 (TCP/IPv4). In the Use the following DNS server addresses: section, enter the IP address of W2K8*xx* as the preferred DNS server.

15. Click OK twice, and then close the Network Connections window.

16. Log off of the odd-numbered computer.

■ PART D: CONFIGURING A PRIMARY ZONE FOR ADATUM.COM ON THE EVEN-NUMBERED COMPUTER

NOTE	Be sure to complete these steps on the even-numbered W2K8*yy* computer on*ly!*

1. Log on to the even-numbered W2K8*yy* computer. Click Start→Administrative Tools→DNS. Expand the DNS MMC to full screen if necessary.

2. Navigate to W2K8*yy*→Forward Lookup Zones.

3. Right-click Forward Lookup Zones, and click New Zone…. Click Next. The Zone Type screen appears.

4. Ensure that the Primary zone radio button is selected, and then click Next.

5. The Zone Name screen appears. In the Zone name: text box, key **adatum.com**. Click Next.

6. The Zone File screen appears. Accept the default selection, and click Next.

Question 8	*What is the default selection on the Zone File screen?*

7. The Dynamic Update screen appears. Accept the default selection of "Do not allow dynamic updates," and click Next.

8. Click Finish. Confirm that adatum.com appears in the list of Forward Lookup Zones configured on W2K8*yy*.

9. Select the adatum.com forward lookup zone.

10. Right-click adatumcontoso.com, and click New Host (A or AAAA)….

11. The New Host screen appears. In the Name (uses parent domain name if blank): text box, enter **W2K8*yy***. In the IP address: text box, enter the IP address of the W2K8*xx* server.

12. Click Add Host. Click OK, and then click Done to confirm. Confirm that an A record has been added for W2K8*yy*.

13. If the Server Manager console is not open already, click Start→Server Manager. View Network Connections.

14. Right-click Local Area Connection, and click Properties. Double-click Internet Protocol Version 4 (TCP/IPv4). In the Use the following DNS server addresses: section, enter the IP address of W2K8*yy* as the preferred DNS server.

15. Click OK twice, and then close the Network Connections window.

16. Log off of the even-numbered computer.

Exercise 4.2	Configuring a Secondary Zone and Zone Transfers
Overview	You have configured a server to host a primary DNS zone for the contoso.com and adatum.com DNS domains. You must now configure these servers so that clients in each domain can resolve a fully qualified domain name (FQDN) in their own domain as well as FQDNs in the remote domain.
Outcomes	After completing this exercise, you will know how to: ▲ Create secondary DNS zones ▲ Configure DNS zone transfers
Completion time	25 minutes
Precautions	This exercise will be performed on both the odd-numbered W2K8*xx* computer and the even-numbered W2K8*yy* computer.

■ **PART A: CONFIGURING THE ODD-NUMBERED DNS SERVER TO ALLOW ZONE TRANSFERS TO THE EVEN-NUMBERED DNS SERVER**

1. Log on to the W2K8*xx* computer. Click the Start button, then click Administrative Tools, and then click DNS.

2. Select the W2K8*xx* node, and then expand the Forward Lookup Zones node. Select the contoso.com node. Right-click on the contoso.com node, and select Properties.

3. On the Zone Transfers tab, place a checkmark next to Allow zone transfers.

4. Select the Only to the following servers radio button, and then click Edit.

5. In the IP addresses of the secondary servers section, key the IP address of W2K8*yy*. Press Enter, and click OK. If you plan to complete the optional Server Core exercise, key the IP address of CORE*xx*. Press Enter, and click OK.

6. Log off of the W2K8*xx* computer.

■ PART B: CONFIGURING THE EVEN-NUMBERED DNS SERVER TO ALLOW ZONE TRANSFERS TO THE ODD-NUMBERED DNS SERVER.

1. Log on to the W2K8*yy* computer. Click the Start button, then click Administrative Tools, and then click DNS.

2. Select the W2K8*yy* node, and then expand the Forward Lookup Zones node. Select the adatum.com node. Right-click on the adatum.com node, and select Properties.

3. On the Zone Transfers tab, place a checkmark next to Allow zone transfers.

4. Select the Only to the following servers radio button, and then click Edit.

5. In the IP addresses of the secondary servers section, key the IP address for the W2K8*xx* server, and press Enter. (If you plan to complete the optional Server Core exercise, also key the IP address of the CORE*xx* server, and press Enter.), Click OK twice.

6. Log off of the W2K8*yy* computer.

■ PART C: CONFIGURING A SECONDARY ZONE FOR ADATUM.COM ON THE ODD-NUMBERED SERVER

1. Log on to the odd-numbered W2K8*xx* computer. Click Start→Administrative Tools→DNS. Expand the DNS MMC to full screen if necessary.

2. Expand the Forward Lookup Zones node.

Question 9	*What forward lookup zones are currently configured on the W2K8xx computer?*

3.   Right-click the Forward Lookup Zones node, and select New Zone…. Click Next to dismiss the initial Welcome screen.

4.   On the Zone Type screen, select Secondary Zone, and click Next.

5.   The Zone Name zone screen appears. Enter **adatum.com**. Click Next.

6.   The Master DNS Servers screen appears. Enter the IP address of the W2K8*yy* server, and press Enter. Confirm that it shows a green checkmark next to the IP address and a value of "OK" in the Validated column. Click Next, and then Finish.

7.   Expand the zone for adatum.com, and confirm that you can see an A record for W2K8*yy*.

NOTE	*If you receive an error when you open the secondary zone, wait a few minutes and press F5.*

8.   Log off of the odd-numbered W2K8*xx* computer.

■ PART D: CONFIGURING A SECONDARY ZONE FOR ADATUM.COM ON THE EVEN-NUMBERED SERVER

1.   Log on to the odd-numbered W2K8*yy* computer. Click Start→Administrative Tools→DNS. Expand the DNS MMC to full screen if necessary.

2.   Expand the Forward Lookup Zones node.

Question 10	*What forward lookup zones are currently configured on the W2K8xx computer?*

3.   Right-click the Forward Lookup Zones node, and select New Zone…. Click Next to dismiss the initial Welcome screen.

4.   On the Zone Type screen, select Secondary Zone, and click Next.

5.   The Zone Name zone screen appears. Enter **contoso.com**. Click Next.

6.   The Master DNS Servers screen appears. Enter the IP address of the W2K8*xx* server, and press Enter. Confirm that it shows a green checkmark next to the IP

address and a value of "OK" in the Validated column. Click Next, and then Finish.

7. Expand the zone for contoso.com, and confirm that you can see an A record for W2K8*xx*.

NOTE	*If you receive an error when you open the secondary zone, wait a few minutes and press F5.*

8. Log off of the even-numbered W2K8*yy* computer.

Exercise 4.3	Configuring Reverse Lookup Zones and Confirming DNS Functionality
Overview	You have configured a server to host primary and secondary DNS zones for the contoso.com and adatum.com DNS domains. You must now confirm that DNS is functioning correctly on each server. To use troubleshooting tools such as nslookup, you will also need to configure a reverse lookup zone for each DNS server.
Outcomes	After completing this exercise, you will know how to: ▲ Create reverse lookup zones ▲ Testing DNS name resolution (nslookup)
Completion time	25 minutes
Precautions	This exercise will be performed on both the odd-numbered W2K8*xx* computer and the even-numbered W2K8*yy* computer.

■ PART A: CONFIGURING A REVERSE LOOKUP ZONE ON THE ODD-NUMBERED W2K8*XX* COMPUTER

1. Log on to the W2K8*xx* computer. Click the Start button, followed by Administrative Tools, followed by DNS.

2. Click the W2K8*xx* zone, and then click the Reverse Lookup Zones node.

Question 11	*What reverse lookup zones are currently configured on the W2K8xx computer?*

3. To create a reverse lookup zone, right-click Reverse Lookup Zones in the left-hand pane, and click New Zone....

4. The New Zone Wizard appears. Click Next to dismiss the initial Welcome screen.

5. The Zone Type screen appears. Click Primary zone, and click Next.

6. The Reverse Lookup Zone Name screen appears. Select IPv4 Reverse Lookup Zone, and click Next.

7. Enter the Network ID of your lab network; this value will be 192.168.1 or the value provided by your instructor or lab proctor. Click Next.

8. The Zone File screen appears. Accept the default value, and click Next.

9. The Dynamic Update screen appears. Accept the default selection of "Do not allow dynamic updates," and click Next.

10. Click Finish. Confirm that the Reverse Lookup Zone appears in the DNS management console.

11. Log off of the W2K8*xx* computer.

■ PART B: CONFIGURING A REVERSE LOOKUP ZONE ON THE EVEN-NUMBERED W2K8 *YY* COMPUTER

1. Log on to the W2K8*yy* computer. Click the Start button, followed by Administrative Tools, followed by DNS.

2. Click the W2K8*yy* zone, and then click the Reverse Lookup Zones node.

Question 12	*What reverse lookup zones are currently configured on the W2K8yy computer?*

3. To create a reverse lookup zone, right-click Reverse Lookup Zones in the left-hand pane, and click New Zone....

4. The New Zone Wizard appears. Click Next to bypass the initial Welcome screen.

5. The Zone Type screen appears. Click Primary zone, and click Next.

6. The Reverse Lookup Zone Name screen appears. Select IPv4 Reverse Lookup Zone, and click Next.

7. Enter the Network ID of your lab network; this value will be 192.168.1 or the value provided by your instructor or lab provider. Click Next.

8. The Zone File screen appears. Accept the default value, and click Next.

9. The Dynamic Update screen appears. Accept the default selection of "Do not allow dynamic updates," and click Next.

10. Click Finish. Confirm that the Reverse Lookup Zone appears in the DNS management console.

11. Log off of the W2K8*yy* computer.

■ PART C: SIMULATING A DATA CHANGE AND PERFORMING A ZONE TRANSFER FOR THE CONTOSO.COM ZONE

1. Log on to the W2K8*xx* computer. Click the Start button, then click Administrative Tools, and then click DNS.

2. Expand the W2K8*xx* node, and then expand the Forward Lookup Zones node.

3. Click the contoso.com node, then right-click and select New Host (A or AAAA)….

4. The New Host screen appears. In the Name (uses parent domain name if blank): text box, enter **test*xx***. In the IP address: text box, enter the IP address assigned to you for test*xx*.

5. Click Add Host. Click OK, and then click Done to confirm. Confirm that an A record has been added for test*xx*.

6. Log off of the W2K8xx computer.

7. Log on to the W2K8*yy* computer. Click the Start button, then click Administrative Tools, and then click DNS.

8. Expand the W2K8*yy* node, and then expand the Forward Lookup Zones node.

9. Right-click the contoso.com node, then right-click and select Transfer from Master.

Question 13	*What happens to the green "Refresh" button in the DNS MMC when you click "Transfer From Master?"*

10. Wait a few minutes, and then press F5 to refresh your view of the contoso.com zone. Confirm that the test*xx* record appears.

11. Log off of the even-numbered computer.

■ PART D: SIMULATING A DATA CHANGE AND PERFORMING A ZONE TRANSFER FOR THE ADATUM.COM ZONE

1. Log on to the W2K8*yy* computer. Click the Start button, then click Administrative Tools, and then click DNS.

2. Expand the W2K8*yy* node, and then expand the Forward Lookup Zones node.

3. Click the adatum.com zone, then right-click and select New Host (A or AAAA)....

4. The New Host screen appears. In the Name (uses parent domain name if blank): text box, enter **test*yy***. In the IP address: text box, enter the IP address assigned to you for test*yy*.

5. Click Add Host. Click OK, and then click Done to confirm. Confirm that an A record has been added for test*yy*.

6. Log off of the W2K8*yy* computer.

7. Log on to the W2K8*xx* computer. Click the Start button, then click Administrative Tools, and then click NS.

8. Expand the W2K8*xx* node, and then expand the Forward Lookup Zones node.

9. Click the adatum.com node, then right-click and select Transfer from Master.

10. Wait a few minutes, and then click press F5 to refresh your view of the contoso.com zone. Confirm that the test*yy* record appears.

11. Log off of the odd-numbered computer.

■ PART E: CONFIRMING DNS FUNCTIONALITY ON THE ODD-NUMBERED COMPUTER

1. Log on to the odd-numbered W2K8*xx* computer. Open a command-prompt window.

2. At the command prompt, key **nslookup w2k8*yy*.adatum.com**, and press Enter. Confirm that the nslookup output matches the A record.

3. At the command prompt, key **nslookup test*yy*.adatum.com**, and press Enter. Confirm that the nslookup output matches the A record that you created in Part D.

4. Log off of the odd-numbered W2K8*xx* computer.

■ **PART F: CONFIRMING DNS FUNCTIONALITY ON THE EVEN-NUMBERED COMPUTER**

1. Log on to the even-numbered W2K8*yy* computer. Open a command-prompt window.

2. At the command prompt, key **nslookup w2k8*xx*.contoso.com**, and press Enter. Confirm that the nslookup output is correct.

3. At the command prompt, key **nslookup test*xx*.contoso.com**, and press Enter. Confirm that the nslookup output is correct.

4. Log off of the even-numbered W2K8*yy* computer.

Exercise 4.4 (optional)	Installing and Configuring the DNS Server Role on Server Core
Overview	To increase the security of servers deployed in several remote offices, you have prepared servers running the Windows Server 2008 Server Core installation option to provide infrastructure services to these offices. You must now prepare one of these servers to function as a DNS server.
Outcomes	After completing this exercise, you will know how to: ▲ Install the DNS Server role on Windows Server 2008 Server Core ▲ Create secondary DNS zones from the command line ▲ Create DNS host (A) records from the command line
Completion time	30 minutes
Precautions	N/A

■ **PART A: INSTALLING AND CONFIGURING THE DNS SERVER ROLE ON SERVER CORE**

1. Press Ctrl+Alt+Delete on the CORE*xx* Windows Server 2008 Server Core computer assigned to you, and log on as the default administrator of the local

computer. Your username will be Administrator. The password will be MSPress#1 or the password that your instructor or lab proctor assigns to you.

2. From the command prompt window, key **start /w ocsetup DNS-Server-Core-Role,** and then press Enter.

3. Key **sc config dns start= auto**, and press Enter.

> **NOTE** *Be sure to include the space between "'=" and "auto" or else the command will fail.*

4. Key net **start dns**, and press Enter.

> **NOTE** *If you receive an error message that the service has already been started, continue to the next step.*

5. To configure the Server Core computer to point to itself for name resolution, key **netsh int ipv4 add dnsserver "Local Area Connection" <IP Address of CORExx>**, and then press Enter.

■ PART B: CONFIGURING A SECONDARY ZONE FOR CONTOSO.COM AND ADATUM.COM AND FORCING A ZONE TRANSFER

1. At the command prompt, key **dnscmd /zoneadd contoso.com /secondary <IP Address of W2K8xx>,** and press Enter.

2. At the command prompt, key **dnscmd /zonerefresh contoso.com**, and press Enter.

3. At the command prompt, key **dnscmd /zoneadd adatum.com /secondary <IP Address of W2K8yy>,** and press Enter.

4. At the command prompt, key **dnscmd /zonerefresh adatum.com**, and press Enter.

■ PART C: CONFIGURING A REVERSE LOOKUP ZONE

1. At the command prompt, key **dnscmd /zoneadd <Network ID>.in-addr. /primary**.

2. Press Enter.

■ PART D: CONFIRMING DNS FUNCTIONALITY

1. At the command prompt, key n**slookup w2k8xx.contoso.com**, and press Enter. Confirm that the nslookup output is correct.

2. At the command prompt, key **nslookup testxx.contoso.com**, and press Enter. Confirm that the nslookup output is correct.

3. At the command prompt, key **nslookup w2k8yy.adatum.com**, and press Enter. Confirm that the nslookup output is correct.

4. At the command prompt, key **nslookup testyy.adatum.com**, and press Enter. Confirm that the nslookup output is correct.

5. Log off of the CORExx computer.

LAB REVIEW QUESTIONS

Completion time	15 minutes

1. In your own words, describe what you learned by completing this lab.

2. You are able to resolve the names of the W2K8xx, W2K8yy, and CORExx computers. Are you able to ping these computers? Why or why not?

3. You want to have only secure dynamic updates for a DNS zone file. Which type of zone file must you have?

4. When do you use forwarding with DNS? Give one example.

5. What is the difference between forwarding and conditional forwarding?

LAB CHALLENGE: CONFIGURING DNS FORWARDERS

Completion time	15 minutes

You have completed testing the DNS server service role on multiple Windows Server 2008 computers using primary and secondary zones. You wish to test the use of DNS forwarders because these will need to be used in several remote offices that rely on a local ISP to perform Internet DNS queries.

After completing this exercise, you will know how to:

▲ Delete a DNS zone

▲ Configure a DNS forwarder

Precautions: If you do not complete the Lab Challenge exercise, you must still complete the Lab Cleanup steps prior to continuing on to Lab 5.

Delete the secondary zone that has been configured on the W2K8*xx* and W2K8*yy* servers. On the W2K8*xx* server, configure a DNS forwarder to the W2K8*yy* server, and then confirm that name resolution for both domains is still successful from W2K8*xx*. On the W2K8*yy* server, configure a conditional forwarder for the contoso.com domain to the W2K*xx* server, and then confirm that name resolution for both domains is still successful from W2K8*yy*.

LAB CLEANUP

Completion time	15 minutes

You have completed testing of the DNS server role, and now need to reset your Windows Server 2008 computers to their original state prior to performing testing of additional infrastructure services that you are planning to deploy to your production network.

After completing this exercise, you will know how to:

▲ Remove the DNS Server role

PART A: REMOVING THE DNS SERVER ROLE FROM W2K8*XX*

1. Log on to the W2K8*xx* server. If the Server Manager console does not appear automatically, click the Start button, and then click Server Manager.

2. In the left-hand pane of Server Manager, click Roles. In the right-hand pane, click Remove Roles. Click Next

3. The Remove Server Roles screen appears. Remove the checkmark next to DNS Server, and then click Next.

4. Click Remove, and then click Close when the removal has completed.

5. When prompted, reboot the W2K8*xx* computer.

6. Log on to the W2K8*xx* server after it reboots. The Server Manager console will reappear automatically. Click Finish when prompted.

7. Log off of the W2K8*xx* server.

PART B: REMOVING THE DNS SERVER ROLE FROM W2K8*YY*

1. Log on to the W2K8*yy* computer. If Server Manager does not appear automatically, click the Start button, and then click Server Manager.

2. In the left-hand pane of Server Manager, click Roles. In the right-hand pane, click Remove Roles. Click Next

3. The Remove Server Roles screen appears. Remove the checkmark next to DNS Server, and then click Next.

4. Click Remove, and then click Close when the removal has completed.

5. When prompted, reboot the W2K8*yy* computer.

6. Log on to the W2K8*yy* server after it reboots. The Server Manager console will reappear automatically. Click Finish when prompted.

PART C: REMOVING THE DNS SERVER ROLE FROM CORE*XX*

1. Log on to the CORE*xx* server. From the command prompt, key **start /w ocsetup DNS-Server-Core-Role /uninstall**, and press Enter.

2. When prompted, click Yes to restart the server.

LAB 5
CONFIGURING ROUTING AND REMOTE ACCESS (RRAS)

This lab contains the following exercises and activities:

Exercise 5.1   Managing the Windows Routing Table

Exercise 5.2   Installing the Routing and Remote Access Role

Exercise 5.3   Configuring Virtual Private Networking

Exercise 5.4   Configuring NPS Network Policies

Lab Review   Questions

Lab Challenge   Working with Delayed Start Services in Windows Server 2008

Lab Cleanup

BEFORE YOU BEGIN

Lab 5 assumes that setup has been completed as specified in the setup document and that your computer has connectivity to other lab computers and the Internet. The required exercises in Lab 5 also assume that you have completed the exercises in Lab 2.

The instructor PC is preconfigured as a domain controller in the lucernepublishing.com domain for demonstration purposes and is named INSTRUCTOR01.

> **NOTE**
>
> *In this lab manual, you will see the characters xx, yy, and zz. These directions assume that you are working on computers configured in pairs and that each computer has a number. One number is odd, and the other number is even. For example, W2K801 is the odd-numbered computer, and W2K802 is the even-numbered computer. When you see xx, substitute the unique number assigned to the odd-numbered computer. When you see yy, substitute the unique number assigned to the even-numbered computer. When you see zz, substitute the number assigned to the computer that you are working at, either odd or even.*

The two Windows Server 2008 server computers referenced in this lab will each be configured with two static IP addresses. For ease of reference, record the two static IP addresses of each server that you will be working with in this lab. We will list exemplar IP addresses that we will reference throughout the lab exercises for clarity:

W2K8*xx*: (For example: W2K801)

NIC 1

IP Address: ___.___.___.___ (192.168.10.1)

Subnet Mask: ___.___.___.___ (255.255.255.0)

Default Gateway: ___.___.___.___ (N/A)

NIC 2

IP Address: ___.___.___.___ (192.168.11.1)

Subnet Mask: ___.___.___.___ (255.255.255.0)

Default Gateway: ___.___.___.___ (N/A)

W2K8*yy*: (For example: W2K802)

NIC 1

IP Address: ___.___.___.___ (192.168.11.2)

Subnet Mask: ___.___.___.___ (255.255.255.0)

Default Gateway: ___.___.___.___ (N/A)

NIC 2

IP Address: ___.___.___.___ (192.168.12.2)

Subnet Mask: ___.___.___.___ (255.255.255.0)

Default Gateway: ___.___.___.___ (N/A)

SCENARIO

You are a network administrator for Contoso, Ltd. Recently, Lucerne Publishing has opened a new office in an adjacent building that needs to be connected to the existing Lucerne Publishing network. In addition, management has expressed a desire to allow home-based staff members to access corporate resources securely using their residential Internet connections. You have installed several Windows Server 2008 computers to test the various components of the Routing and Remote Access service.

After completing this lab, you will be able to:

- Manage the Windows Routing Table

- Install the Routing and Remote Access Role

- Configure Virtual Private Networking

- Configure NPS Network Polices

Estimated lab time: 140 minutes

Exercise 5.1	Managing the Windows Routing Table
Overview	You have just procured multiple servers to route traffic between multiple networks. You now need to configure IP addresses on these computers that simulate a routed network and test the ability for traffic to be routed between the servers automatically.
Outcomes	After completing this exercise, you will know how to: ▲ Configure multiple Network Interface Cards ▲ Test connectivity between IPv4 subnets ▲ Configure Windows Firewall exceptions
Completion time	20 minutes
Precautions	This exercise will be performed on both the odd-numbered W2K8*xx* computer and the even-numbered W2K8*yy* computer.

■ PART A: CONFIGURING STATIC IP ADDRESSES ON NIC1 AND NIC2 OF THE ODD-NUMBERED W2K8*XX* COMPUTER

1. Press Ctrl+Alt+Delete on the W2K8*xx* Windows Server 2008 computer assigned to you, and log on as the default administrator of the local computer. Your username will be Administrator. The password will be MSPress#1 or the password that your instructor or lab proctor assigns to you.

2. If the Initial Configuration Tasks (ICT) screen window opens automatically, place a checkmark next to Do not show this window at logon, and click Close.

3. If the Server Manager window does not appear automatically, click the Start button, and then click Server Manager.

4. Click View Network Connections. The Network Connections window is displayed.

Question 1	*What are the names of the network connections installed on this computer?*

5. Right-click Local Area Connection, and select Properties. The network connection's Properties window will be displayed.

6. Click Internet Protocol Version 4 (TCP/IPv4), and select Properties. The Internet Protocol Version 4 (TCP/IPv4) Properties window will be displayed.

7. Select the Use the following IP address: radio button. Enter the following IP address information for the NIC1 IP address that you recorded at the beginning of this lab.

   IP Address: for example, 192.168.10.1

   Subnet Mask: for example, 255.255.255.0

   Default Gateway: N/A

8. Click OK, and then click Close two times to save your changes.

9. Right-click Local Area Connection 2, and select Properties. The network connection's Properties window will be displayed.

10. Click Internet Protocol Version 4 (TCP/IPv4), and select Properties. The Internet Protocol Version 4 (TCP/IPv4) Properties window will be displayed.

11. Select the Use the following IP address: radio button. Enter the following IP address information for the NIC2 IP address that you recorded at the beginning of this lab.

    IP Address: for example, 192.168.11.1

    Subnet Mask: for example, 255.255.255.0

    Default Gateway: N/A

Question 2	Have you configured the two NICs on the same subnet or on different subnets? How can you tell?

12. Click OK, and then click Close to save your changes.

13. Close the Network Connections window.

■ PART B: CONFIGURING A WINDOWS FIREWALL EXCEPTION TO ALLOW PING CONNECTIVITY

1. Click Start→Administrative Tools→Windows Firewall with Advanced Security.

2. The Windows Firewall with Advanced Security screen appears. Click Inbound Rules.

3. Right-click Inbound Rules, and click New Rule....

4. The Rule Type screen appears. Select the Custom radio button, and click Next.

5. The Program screen appears. Select the All programs radio button, and click Next.

6. The Protocols and Ports screen appears. In the Protocol type: drop-down box, select ICMPv4, and click Next.

7. The Scope screen appears. Accept the default values, and then click Next.

8. The Action screen appears. Accept the default value, and then click Next.

9. The Profile screen appears. Accept the default value, and then click Next.

10. The Name screen appears. In the Name: text box, key **Allow Lab Ping**, and click Finish.

11. Confirm that the Allow Lab Ping rule appears with a green checkbox next to it, and close the Windows Firewall with Advanced Security screen.

12. Log off of the odd-numbered computer.

■ PART C: CONFIGURING STATIC IP ADDRESSES ON NIC1 AND NIC2 OF THE EVEN-NUMBERED W2K8YY COMPUTER

1. Press Ctrl+Alt+Delete on the W2K8*yy* Windows Server 2008 computer assigned to you, and log on as the default administrator of the local computer. Your username will be Administrator. The password will be MSPress#1 or the password that your instructor or lab proctor assigns to you.

2. If the ICT screen window opens automatically, place a checkmark next to Do not show this window at logon, and click Close.

3. If the Server Manager window does not appear automatically, click the Start button, and then click Server Manager.

4. Click View Network Connections. The Network Connections window is displayed.

5. Right-click Local Area Connection, and select Properties. The network connection's Properties window will be displayed.

6. Click Internet Protocol Version 4 (TCP/IPv4), and select Properties. The Internet Protocol Version 4 (TCP/IPv4) Properties window will be displayed.

7. Select the Use the following IP address: radio button. Enter the following IP address information for the instructor computer that you recorded at the beginning of this lab.

   IP Address: for example, 192.168.11.2

   Subnet Mask: for example, 255.255.255.0

   Default Gateway: N/A

8. Click OK, and then click Close two times to save your changes.

9. Right-click Local Area Connection 2, and select Properties. The network connection's Properties window will be displayed.

10. Click Internet Protocol Version 4 (TCP/IPv4), and select Properties. The Internet Protocol Version 4 (TCP/IPv4) Properties window will be displayed.

11. Select the Use the following IP address: radio button. Enter the following IP address information for the instructor computer that you recorded at the beginning of this lab.

   IP Address: for example, 192.168.12.2

   Subnet Mask: for example, 255.255.255.0

   Default Gateway: N/A

12. Click OK, and then click Close to save your changes.

13. Close the Network Connections window.

■ PART D: CONFIGURING A WINDOWS FIREWALL EXCEPTION TO TEST PING CONNECTIVITY

1. Click Start→Administrative Tools→Windows Firewall with Advanced Security.

2. The Windows Firewall with Advanced Security screen appears. Click Inbound Rules.

3. Right-click Inbound Rules, and click New Rule....

4. The Rule Type screen appears. Click Select the Custom radio button, and click Next.

5. The Program screen appears. Click Select the All programs radio button, and click Next.

6. The Protocols and Ports screen appears. In the Protocol type: drop-down box, select ICMPv4, and click Next.

7. The Scope screen appears. Accept the default values, and then click Next.

8. The Action screen appears. Accept the default value, and then click Next.

9. The Profile screen appears. Accept the default value, and then click Next.

10. The Name screen appears. In the Name: text box, key **Allow Lab Ping**, and click Finish.

11. Confirm that the Allow Lab Ping rule appears with a green checkbox next to it, and close the Windows Firewall with Advanced Security screen.

12. Log off of the odd-numbered computer.

■ PART E: TESTING TCP/IP CONNECTIVITY ON THE ODD-NUMBERED COMPUTER

1. Log on to the odd-numbered W2K8*xx* computer. Open a command-prompt window.

2. Ping the IP address assigned to NIC1 of the odd-numbered computer. For example, key **ping 192.168.10.1**, and then press Enter.

> | Question 3 | Do you receive a ping response? Why or why not? |

3. Ping the IP address assigned to NIC2 of the odd-numbered computer. For example, key **ping 192.168.11.1**, and then press Enter.

> | Question 4 | Do you receive a ping response? Why or why not? |

4. Ping the IP address assigned to NIC1 of the even-numbered computer. For example, key **ping 192.168.11.2**, and then press Enter.

> | Question 5 | Do you receive a ping response? Why or why not? |

5. Ping the IP address assigned to NIC2 of the even-numbered computer. For example, key **ping 192.168.12.2**, and then press Enter.

> | Question 6 | Do you receive a ping response? Why or why not? |

6. Log off of the odd-numbered computer.

■ PART F: TESTING TCP/IP CONNECTIVITY ON THE EVEN-NUMBERED COMPUTER

1. Log on to the even-numbered W2K8*yy* computer. Open a command-prompt window.

2. Ping the IP address assigned to NIC1 of the even-numbered computer. For example, key **ping 192.168.11.2**, and then press Enter.

Question 7	Do you receive a ping response? Why or why not?

3. Ping the IP address assigned to NIC2 of the even-numbered computer. For example, key **ping 192.168.12.2**, and then press Enter.

Question 8	Do you receive a ping response? Why or why not?

4. Ping the IP address assigned to NIC2 of the odd-numbered computer. For example, key **ping 192.168.11.1**, and then press Enter.

Question 9	Do you receive a ping response? Why or why not?

5. Ping the IP address assigned to NIC1 of the odd-numbered computer. For example, **key ping 192.168.10.1**, and then press Enter.

Question 10	Do you receive a ping response? Why or why not?

6. Log off of the even-numbererd computer.

Exercise 5.2	Installing the Routing and Remote Access Role
Overview	You have configured multiple networks in a lab to simulate the opening of the new Lucerne Publishing office. You must now configure routing between networks to allow for full network connectivity.
Outcomes	After completing this exercise, you will know how to: ▲ Install the Routing and Remote Access Server role ▲ Configure Static Routing
Completion time	25 minutes
Precautions	This exercise will be performed on both the odd-numbered and even-numbered computers.

■ PART A: INSTALLING THE ROUTING AND REMOTE ACCESS SERVER ROLE SERVICE ON THE ODD- AND EVEN-NUMBERED COMPUTERS

> **NOTE** *Part A of this exercise must be completed on both computers before continuing.*

1. Press Ctrl+Alt+Delete on the W2K8*zz* Windows Server 2008 computer assigned to you, and log on as the default administrator of the local computer. Your username will be Administrator. The password will be MSPress#1 or the password that your instructor or lab proctor assigns to you.

2. If the Initial Configuration Tasks (ICT) screen window opens automatically, place a checkmark next to Do not show this window at logon, and click Close.

3. If the Server Manager window does not appear automatically, click the Start button, and then click Server Manager.

4. In the left-hand pane of Server Manager, double-click Roles.

5. Click Add Roles. Click Next to dismiss the initial Welcome screen.

6. The Select Server Roles screen appears. Place a checkmark next to Network Policy and Access Services. Click Next twice to continue.

7. The Select Role Services screen appears. Place a checkmark next to Routing. The Add role services required for Routing screen appears. Click Add Required Role Services.

8. Click Next, then click Install, and then click Close.

9. Click Start→Administrative Tools→Routing and Remote Access. The Routing and Remote Access screen appears.

10. Right-click W2K8*zz* (local), and click Configure and Enable Routing and Remote Access. The Welcome to the Routing and Remote Access Server Setup Wizard screen appears.

11. Click Next. The Configuration screen appears. Select the Custom configuration radio button, and click Next.

12. The Custom Configuration screen appears. Place a checkmark next to LAN Routing, and click Next. Click Finish.

13. The Start the service screen appears. Click Start service.

14.   Confirm that the server name now has a green arrow icon next to it.

15.   Log off of the W2K8*zz* computer.

■ PART B: CONFIGURING LAN ROUTING ON THE ODD-NUMBERED COMPUTER

NOTE	*Part A must be completed on the odd- and even-numbered computers before continuing*

1.   Log on to the odd-numbered W2K8*xx* computer.

2.   Click Start→Administrative Tools→Routing and Remote Access.

3.   Click the plus sign next to W2K8*xx* (local). Click W2K8*xx* (local), and navigate to IPv4→Static Routes.

4.   Right-click Static Routes, and click New Static Route…. The IPv4 Static Route screen appears.

5.   In the Interface: drop-down box, select Local Area Connection 2. In the Destination: text box, enter the network address portion of the IP address assigned to NIC2 of the even-numbered computer, such as 192.168.12.0. In the Network Mask: text box, enter the subnet mask assigned to NIC2 of the even-numbered computer, such as 255.255.255.0. In the Gateway: text box, enter the IP address assigned to NIC2 of the odd-numbered computer, such as 192.168.11.1.

6.   Click OK. Log off of the odd-numbered computer.

■ PART C: CONFIGURING LAN ROUTING ON THE EVEN-NUMBERED COMPUTER

NOTE	*Part A must be completed on both the odd- and even-numbered computers before continuing!*

1.   Log on to the even-numbered W2K8*yy* computer.

2.   Click Start→Administrative Tools→Routing and Remote Access.

3. Click the plus sign next to W2K8*yy* (local). Click W2K8*xx* (local), and navigate to IPv4→Static Routes.

4. Right-click Static Routes, and click New Static Route…. The IPv4 Static Route screen appears.

5. In the Interface: drop-down box, select Local Area Connection. In the Destination: text box, enter the network address portion of the IP address assigned to NIC1 of the odd-numbered computer, such as 192.168.10.0. In the Network Mask: text box, enter the subnet mask assigned to NIC1 of the odd-numbered computer, such as 255.255.255.0. In the Gateway: text box, enter the IP address assigned to NIC1 of the even-numbered computer, such as 192.168.11.2.

6. Click OK. Log off of the even-numbered computer.

■ PART D: TESTING LAN ROUTING

1. Log on to the odd-numbered W2K8*xx* computer. Open a command prompt.

2. Ping the IP address assigned to NIC2 of the even-numbered computer. For example, key **ping 192.168.12.2**, and then press Enter.

Question 11	Do you receive a ping response? Why or why not?

3. Log off of the odd-numbered W2K8*xx* computer.

4. Log on,to the even-numbered W2K8*yy* computer. Open a command prompt.

5. Ping the IP address assigned to NIC1 of the odd-numbered computer. For example, key **ping 192.168.10.1**, and then press Enter.

Question 12	Do you receive a ping response? Why or why not?

6. Log off of the even-numbered W2K8*xx* computer.

Exercise 5.3	Configuring Virtual Private Networking
Overview	Lucerne Publishing management has expressed a desire to allow remote access connectivity to home-based staff members using their residential Internet connections. You have procured a Windows Server 2008 server to configure as a Virtual Private Networking (VPN) server. In this exercise, you will remove the previously configured LAN routing configuration and then configure the Windows Server 2008 computer to accept incoming VPN connections.
Outcomes	After completing this exercise, you will know how to: ▲ Configure a Windows Server 2008 VPN server
Completion time	25 minutes
Precautions	This exercise will be performed on the odd-numbered W2K8*xx* computer.

1.   Log on to the W2K8*xx* computer. Click the Start button, followed by Administrative Tools, followed by Routing and Remote Access.

2.   Right-click W2K8*xx* (local), and click Disable Routing and Remote Access. Click Yes to acknowledge the warning that appears.

3.   Right-click W2K8*xx* (local), and click Configure and Enable Routing and Remote Access. The Welcome to the Routing and Remote Access Server Setup Wizard screen appears.

4.   Click Next. The Configuration screen appears. Select the Remote access (dial-up or VPN) radio button, and click Next.

5.   The Remote Access screen appears. Place a checkmark next to VPN, and click Next.

6.   The VPN Connection screen appears. Select Local Area Connection 2, and click Next.

7.   The IP Address Assignment screen appears. Click the From a specified range of addresses, and click Next.

8.   The Address Range Assignment screen appears. Click New. The New IPv4 Address Range screen appears. In the Start IP Address: text box, enter a starting IP address for a range to be issued to your VPN clients, such as 10.10.10.1. In the End IP Address: text box, enter an ending IP address to be issued to your VPN clients, such as 10.10.10.50.

9.   Click OK, and then click Next.

10. The Managing Multiple Remote Access Servers screen appears. Accept the default value.

11. Click Next, and then click Finish. Click OK to acknowledge the warning message that appears.

12. Log off of the W2K8xx computer.

Exercise 5.4	Configuring NPS Network Policies
Overview	To test VPN connectivity to the Lucerne Publishing network, you have decided to allow remote access to local Administrators of the VPN server.
Outcomes	After completing this exercise, you will know how to: ▲ Configure an NPS Network Policy to control access to a Windows Server 2008 VPN server
Completion time	25 minutes
Precautions	This exercise will be performed on the odd-numbered W2K8xx computer only.

1. Press Ctrl+Alt+Delete on the W2K8xx odd-numbered computer assigned to you, and log on as the default administrator of the local computer. Your username will be Administrator. The password will be MSPress#1 or the password that your instructor or lab proctor assigns to you.

2. Click Start→Administrative Tools→Network Policy Server.

3. The Network Policy Server window appears. Drill down to Policies→Network Policies.

Question 13	What Network Policies are configured by default?
Question 14	What Access type is configured for these policies?

4. Right-click Network policies, and click New.

5. The New Network Policy screen appears. In the Policy Name text box, enter **Allow Administrators Remote Access.**

6. In the Type of network access server drop-down box, select Remote Access Server (VPN-Dialup), and click Next.

7. The Specify Conditions screen appears. Click Add.... The Select condition screen appears.

Question 15	Name three types of conditions that you can add to a Network Policy

8. Click Select Windows Groups, and then click Add....

9. The Windows Groups screen appears. Click Add Groups....

10. The Select Groups screen appears. Key **Administrators**, and click OK.

11. Click OK, and then click Next to continue.

12. The Specify Access Permission screen appears. Accept the Access granted default radio button, and click Next.

13. The Configure Authentication Methods screen appears.

Question 16	What are the default authentication methods that are selected?

14. Accept the default authentication methods, and click Next.

15. The Configure Constraints screen appears. Select the Idle Timeout constraint. In the right-hand pane, place a checkmark next to Disconnect after the maximum idle time. Enter a maximum idle time of 15 minutes. Click Next.

16. The Configure Settings screen appears. Accept the default selections. Click Next, and then click Finish.

17. Log off of the W2K8*xx* computer.

LAB REVIEW QUESTIONS

Completion time	15 minutes

1. In your own words, describe what you learned by completing this lab.

2. When creating a Network Policy, what are the built-in constraints that you can define?

3. If multiple network policies exist that match a particular user's connection attempt, which one will be applied?

4. What is the default mechanism for auditing remote access connections?

LAB CHALLENGE: WORKING WITH DELAYED START SERVICES IN WINDOWS SERVER 2008

Completion time	15 minutes

You have completed testing the Routing and Remote Access server role on multiple Windows Server 2008 computers using primary and secondary zones. You wish to test the configuration of the RRAS server role, particularly relating to a new service startup type that you notice in the Services MMC snap-in.

After completing this exercise, you will know how to:

▲ Understand and configure the Delayed Start service mechanism

Precautions: If you do not complete the Lab Challenge exercise, you must still complete the Lab Cleanup steps prior to continuing on to Lab 6.

Reconfigure the Routing and Remote Access service on the W2K8zz computer for LAN routing, as described in Exercise 5.2. Reboot the computer, open the RRAS MMC, and observe the length of time that it takes for a green icon to be displayed next to the server name.

Discuss the "Automatic (Delayed Start)" service startup type in Windows Server 2008, and modify the service so that routing becomes available more quickly when the server is rebooted.

LAB CLEANUP

Completion time	15 minutes

You have completed testing of the Routing and Remote Access server role and now need to reset your Windows Server 2008 computers to their original state prior to performing testing of additional infrastructure services that you are planning to deploy to your production network.

After completing this exercise, you will know how to:

▲ Remove the Routing and Remote Access Server role

■ PART A: REMOVING THE ROUTING AND REMOTE ACCESS SERVER ROLE FROM W2K8*XX*

1. Log on to the W2K8*xx* server. If the Server Manager console does not appear automatically, click the Start button, and then click Server Manager.

2. In the left-hand pane of Server Manager, click Roles. In the right-hand pane, click Remove Roles. Click Next.

3. The Remove Server Roles screen appears. Remove the checkmark next to Network Policy and Access Services, and then click Next.

4. Click Remove, and then click Close when the removal has completed.

5. When prompted, reboot the W2K8*xx* computer.

6. Log on to the W2K8*xx* server after it reboots. The Server Manager console will reappear automatically. Click Finish when prompted.

7. Reconfigure the IP configuration of NIC1 in the W2K8*xx* server to its state at the end of Lab 4.

8. Log off of the W2K8*xx* server.

■ PART B: REMOVING THE ROUTING AND REMOTE ACCESS SERVER ROLE FROM W2K8*YY*

1. Log on to the W2K8*yy* computer. If the Server Manager console does not appear automatically, click the Start button, and then click Server Manager.

2. In the left-hand pane of Server Manager, click Roles. In the right-hand pane, click Remove Roles. Click Next.

3. The Remove Server Roles screen appears. Remove the checkmark next to Network Policy and Access Services, and then click Next.

4. Click Remove, and then click Close when the removal has completed.

5. When prompted, reboot the W2K8*yy* computer.

6. Log on to the W2K8*yy* server after it reboots. The Server Manager console will reappear automatically. Click Finish when prompted.

7. Reconfigure the IP configuration of NIC1 in the W2K8*yy* server to its state at the end of Lab 4.

8. Log off of the W2K8*yy* server.

LAB 6
CONFIGURING FILE SERVICES

This lab contains the following exercises and activities:

Exercise 6.1   Installing the File Server Resource Manager

Exercise 6.2   Creating and Managing Windows File Shares

Exercise 6.3   Configuring DFS-Namespaces

Exercise 6.4   Configuring DFS-Replication

Lab Review   Questions

Lab Challenge 6.1   Configuring a File Screen

Lab Challenge 6.2   Configuring File Shares on Server Core Computer

Lab Cleanup

BEFORE YOU BEGIN

Lab 6 assumes that setup has been completed as specified in the setup document and that your computer has connectivity to other lab computers and the Internet. The required exercises in Lab 6 assume that you have completed the preparatory exercises in Labs 1 and 2. Lab Challenge Exercise 2 assumes that you have completed the optional Server Core exercises in Labs 1 and 2.

The instructor PC is preconfigured as a domain controller in the lucernepublishing.com domain for demonstration purposes and is named INSTRUCTOR01.

> **NOTE**
>
> *In this lab manual, you will see the characters xx, yy, and zz. These directions assume that you are working on computers configured in pairs and that each computer has a number. One number is odd, and the other number is even. For example, W2K801 is the odd-numbered computer, and W2K802 is the even-numbered computer. When you see xx, substitute the unique number assigned to the odd-numbered computer. When you see yy, substitute the unique number assigned to the even-numbered computer. When you see zz, substitute the number assigned to the computer that you are working at, either odd or even.*

The four Windows Server 2008 server computers referenced in this lab will each be configured with static IP addresses. For ease of reference, record the static IP addresses of each server that you will be working with in this lab:

INSTRUCTOR01 (Instructor Computer)

IP Address: ___.___.___.___

Subnet Mask: ___.___.___.___

Default Gateway: ___.___.___.___

W2K8*xx*: (For example: W2K801)

IP Address: ___.___.___.___

Subnet Mask: ___.___.___.___

Default Gateway: ___.___.___.___

W2K8*yy*: (For example: W2K802)

IP Address: ___.___.___.___

Subnet Mask: ___.___.___.___

Default Gateway: ___.___.___.___

CORE*xx*: (For example: CORE01)

IP Address: ___.___.___.___

Subnet Mask: ___.___.___.___

Default Gateway: ___.___.___.___

SCENARIO

You are a network administrator for Lucerne Publishing. Recently, Lucerne Publishing has opened a new office in an adjacent building that has been connected to the existing Lucerne Publishing network. Now that network connectivity has been established, the staff in the new office will require storage for their mission-critical files and databases. Additionally, certain files need to be made available in both offices to users in each location.

After completing this lab, you will be able to:

- Install the File Server Resource Manager

- Create and Manage Windows File Shares

- Configure DFS Namespaces and DFS-Replication

Estimated lab time: 155 minutes

Exercise 6.1	Installing the File Server Resource Manager
Overview	You have just procured multiple servers to act as file servers within your organization. You must prepare these servers to host Distributed File System (DFS) and other advanced functionality available in Windows Server 2008 file servers.
Outcomes	After completing this exercise, you will know how to: ▲ Install the File Server Resource Manager
Completion time	20 minutes
Precautions	This exercise will be performed on both the odd-numbered W2K8*xx* computer and the even-numbered W2K8*yy* computer.

1. Press Ctrl+Alt+Delete on the W2K8*zz* Windows Server 2008 computer assigned to you, and log on as the default administrator of the local computer. Your username will be Administrator. The password will be MSPress#1 or the password that your instructor or lab proctor assigns to you.

2. If the Initial Configuration Tasks (ICT) screen window opens automatically, place a checkmark next to Do not show this window at logon, and click Close.

3. If the Server Manager window does not appear automatically, click the Start button, and then click Server Manager.

4. In the left-hand pane of Server Manager, double-click Roles.

5. Click Add Roles. Click Next to bypass the initial Welcome screen.

6. The Select Server Roles screen appears. Place a checkmark next to File Services. Click Next twice to continue.

7. The Select Role Services screen appears. Confirm that there is a checkmark next to File Server. Place a checkmark next to each of the following, and then click Next:

   - Distributed File System

   - DFS-Namespaces

   - DFS-Replication

   - File Server Resource Manager

8. The Create a DFS Namespace screen appears. Select the Create a namespace later using the DFS Management Snap-In in Server Manager radio button. Click Next.

9. The Configure Storage Usage Monitoring screen appears. Place a checkmark next to Local Disk (C:).

Question 1	*What reports does this screen generate by default?*

10. Click Next. The Set Report Options screen appears.

Question 2	*Where are reports stored by default?*

11. Click Next, and then click Install. Click Close when the installation completes.

12. Log off of the W2K8*zz* computer.

Exercise 6.2	Creating and Managing Windows File Shares
Overview	You have configured two new Windows Server 2008 computers to act as file servers for the new Lucerne Publishing office. You will now configure multiple shared folders, also known as file shares, to test access levels for local users on each computer.
Outcomes	After completing this exercise, you will know how to: ▲ Create local users and groups ▲ Create and manage file shares
Completion time	25 minutes
Precautions	This exercise will be completed using both the even- and odd-numbered computers. Portions will be completed from the odd-numbered computer only; other portions will be completed from the even-numbered computer only.

■ PART A: CREATING LOCAL USERS AND GROUPS ON BOTH W2K8ZZ COMPUTERS

1. Log on to the W2K8*xx* computer. Click the Start button, followed by Administrative Tools, followed by Computer Management.

2. Drill down to Local Users and Groups→Users.

3. Right-click Users, and click New User…. Create a new user with the following information:

   - Username: **W2K8*zz*Test01**

   - Password: **MSPress#1**

   - Remove the "User must change password…" option

4. Create a second user with a username of W2K8*zz*Test02.

5. Right-click Groups, and click New Group…. Create a new group with the following information:

   - Group Name: **W2K8*zz*TestGroup01**

   - Members: **W2K8*zz*Test01**

6. Create a second group with a group name of **W2K8zzTestGroup02**, with **W2K8zzTest02** as a member.

7. Log off of the W2K8zz computer.

■ PART B: CONFIGURING FILE SHARES AND PERMISSIONS ON BOTH W2K8ZZ COMPUTERS

1. Log on to the W2K8zz computer as Administrator.

2. Create the following directories in the root of the C:\ drive:

   - C:\TestFolder01

   - C:\TestFolder02

   - C:\TestFolder03

   - C:\TestFolder04

3. Create an empty text file in each folder corresponding to the name of the folder: TestFile01.txt in C:\TestFolder01, TestFile02.txt in C:\TestFolder02, and so forth.

4. Right-click C:\TestFolder01, and click Share….

5. The File Sharing window appears. In the Choose people to share with text box, enter **W2K8zzTest01**. Click Add.

Question 3	*What is the access level granted to the newly added user?*

6. Click the drop-down box next to Reader.

Question 4	*What are the available access levels that can be granted?*

7. Click Contributor.

8. Click Share. If the Network discovery and file sharing window appears asking whether you want to enable network discovery for all public networks, click No, make the network that I am connected to a private network.

Question 5	What is the UNC path of the newly created share?

9. Click Done.

10. Repeat Steps 4 through 9 to share the TestFolder02 folder. Grant W2K8*zz*Test02 Contributor permissions to the share.

11. Repeat Steps 4 through 9 to share the TestFolder03 folder. Grant W2K8*zz*TestGroup01 Contributor permissions to the share.

12. Repeat Steps 4 through 9 to share the TestFolder04 folder. Grant W2K8*zz*TestGroup2 Contributor permissions to the share.

Question 6	What are the UNC paths of all shares configured on both servers?

■ PART C: CONFIRMING FILE SHARE ACCESS

1. Log on to the W2K8*zz* computer as the local Administrator.

2. Click Start, enter the UNC name of the other computer, and press Enter. For example, if you are logged on to the W2K802 computer, browse to \\W2K801. If you are logged on to the W2K801 computer, browse to \\W2K802.

3. Attempt to browse the contents of the shares on your partner's computer.

Question 7	Why is the local user from one computer able to access resources on the other computer?

4. Log off of the W2K8*zz* computer.

5. Log on to the W2K8*zz* computer as W2K8*zz*Test01.

6. Click Start, and then enter the UNC name of your partner's computer. For example, if you are logged on to the W2K802 computer, browse to \\W2K801. If you are logged on to the W2K801 computer, browse to \\W2K802.

Question 8	Why are you now prompted for a username and password?

7. Enter the username and password of W2K8*zz*Test01 for your partner's computer. For example, if you are attempting to access a share on W2K801, enter the credentials for W2K801Test01. Do *not* select the option to remember these credentials.

8. Attempt to access each shared folder using the W2K8*zz*Test01credentials.

Question 9	Which folders are you able to access and why??

9. Log off of the W2K8*zz* computer.

10. Log on to the W2K8*zz* computer as W2K8*zz*Test02.

11. Click Start, and then enter the UNC name of the other computer. For example, if you are logged on to the W2K802 computer, browse to \\W2K801. If you are logged on to the W2K801 computer, browse to \\W2K802.

12. Enter the username and password of W2K8*zz*Test02 for your partner's computer. For example, if you are attempting to access a share on W2K801, enter the credentials for W2K801Test02. Do *not* select the option to remember these credentials.

13. Attempt to access each shared folder using the W2K8*zz*Test01credentials.

Question 10	Which folders are you able to access?

14. Log off of the W2K8*zz* computer.

Exercise 6.3	Configuring DFS-Namespaces
Overview	Management has expressed a concern that Lucerne Publishing users will have difficulty locating individual files and folders as new servers are added to the network and has asked whether there is any mechanism to simplify this process. You decide to configure a DFS Namespace on the two Windows Server 2008 file servers to test the use of this function to create a single unified namespace for file and folder access.
Outcomes	After completing this exercise, you will know how to: ▲ Configure a DFS Namespace
Completion time	25 minutes
Precautions	This exercise will be performed on the odd-numbered W2K8*xx* computer only.

■ **PART A: CONFIGURING A DFS NAMESPACE ON W2K801**

1. Press Ctrl-Alt-Delete on the W2K8*xx* odd-numbered computer assigned to you, and log on as the default administrator of the local computer. Your username will be Administrator. The password will be MSPress#1 or the password that your instructor or lab proctor assigns to you.

2. Click Start→Administrative Tools→DFS Management.

3. Click Namespaces in the left-hand pane.

4. Right-click Namespaces, and click New Namespace….

5. The Namespace Server screen appears. In the Server: text box, enter **W2K801**, and click Next.

Question 11	*What message do you receive?*

6. Click Yes. The Namespace Name and Settings screen appears.

7. In the Name: text box, enter **Public**.

8. Click Edit Settings.

Question 12	What is the local path of the shared folder?

Question 13	What are the default shared folder permissions?

9. Click OK, and then click Next.

10. The Namespace Type screen appears. Accept the default selection, and click Next, followed by Create. Click Close when the namespace creation is completed.

11. Right-click the newly created namespace, and click New Folder….

12. The New Folder screen appears. In the Name: folder, enter **Folder01**. Click Add.

13. The Add Folder Target screen appears. In the Path to folder target: text box, enter **\\W2K8*xx*\TestFolder01**. Click OK twice.

14. Repeat Steps 11 through 13 to add the remaining shared folders to the DFS Namespace under the name Folder02, Folder03, and Folder04.

15. Log off of the W2K801*xx* computer.

■ PART B: CONFIRMING DFS-NAMESPACE FUNCTIONALITY

1. Log on to the W2K8*yy* computer as W2K8*yy*Test01.

2. Browse to \\W2K8*xx*\Public. When prompted, enter the username and password for W2K8*xx*Test01.

3. Attempt to access each shared folder using the W2K8*xx*Test01 credentials.

Question 14	Which folders are you able to access?

4. Log off of the W2K8*yy* computer.

5. Log on to the W2K8*yy* computer as W2K8*yy*Test02.

6. Browse to \\W2K8*xx*\Public. When prompted, enter the username and password for W2K8*xx*Test02.

7. Attempt to access each shared folder using the W2K8*xx*Test02 credentials.

Question 15	Which folders are you able to access?

8. Log off of the W2K8*yy* computer.

Exercise 6.4	Configuring DFS-Replication
Overview	One of the Lucerne Publishing departments maintains offices in both building locations. This office needs to have certain files and folders accessible in both locations, and any changes made in each location must be reflected for users in the other location. You decide to configure a DFS replication group to test the functionality of the DFS-Replication role service in Windows Server 2008.
Outcomes	After completing this exercise, you will know how to: ▲ Configure a DFS-Replication replication group
Completion time	25 minutes
Precautions	This exercise will be performed on both the odd-numbered W2K8*xx* computer and the even-numbered W2K8*yy* computer.

■ PART A: JOINING THE W2K8ZZ COMPUTERS TO AN ACTIVE DIRECTORY DOMAIN

1. Log on to the W2K8*zz* computer as the local Administrator.

2. Click Start→Administrative Tools→Server Manager. In the Server Summary→Computer Information section, click Change System Properties.

3. The System Properties screen appears.

Question 16	*What is this computer's current domain/workgroup configuration?*

4. Click Change. The computer Name/Domain Changes screen appears.

5. Click the Domain radio button. Key **lucernepublishing.com**, and then click OK.

6. The Windows Security screen appears. Enter the username and password of an administrator in the lucernepublishing.com domain as provided by your instructor or lab proctor, and click OK. The Welcome to the lucernepublishing.com domain screen appears. Click OK twice.

7. Click Close. When prompted, restart the computer.

■ PART B: CREATING FOLDERS TO BE CONFIGURED FOR DFS REPLICATION ON EACH COMPUTER

1. Log on to the W2K8*zz* computer as the Administrator for the lucernepublishing domain.

2. Create a folder in the root of the C:\ drive called Replication. Share this folder as \\W2K8*zz*\Replication. Click the drop-down arrow, and then click Find. Grant the Domain Users group from the lucernepublishing.com domain the Co-owner share permission.

3. Log off of the W2K8*zz* computer.

■ PART C: CONFIGURING DFS REPLICATION ON THE ODD-NUMBERED COMPUTER

1. Log on to the W2K8*xx* odd-numbered computer as an administrator of the lucernepublishing.com domain.

2. Click Start→Administrative Tools→DFS Management.

3. Right-click Replication, and then click New Replication Group….

4.   The Replication Group Type screen appears.

> | **Question 17** | *What types of preconfigured replication groups can you configure?* |
> |---|---|

5.   Click Next. The Name and Domain screen appears. In the Name of replication group: text box, enter **DFSReplication**.

6.   Click Next.

7.   The Replication Group Members screen appears. Click Add.

8.   The Select Computers screen appears. Enter the name of the odd-numbered computer, and then click OK.

9.   Click Add. The Select Computers screen appears again. Enter the name of the even-numbered computer, and then click OK.

10.   The Topology Selection screen appears.

> | **Question 18** | *Why is the hub-and-spoke topology grayed out?* |
> |---|---|

11.   Click Next. The Replication Group Schedule and Bandwidth screen appears. Accept the default selection, and click Next.

12.   The Primary Member screen appears. In the Primary member: drop-down box, select the odd-numbered W2K8*xx* computer.

13.   Click Next. The Folders to Replicate screen appears. Click Add, and specify the C:\Replication folder created in PART B.

14.   Click OK, and then click Next. The Local Path of Replication on Other Members screen appears.

> | **Question 19** | *What member server and local path are configured?* |
> |---|---|

15. Click Edit. Set the status of the even-numbered computer to Enabled, and specify the Local path as C:\Replication.

16. Click OK, followed by Next, followed by Create.

17. Click OK. The Replication Delay screen appears. Read the warning message, and then click OK.

■ PART D: TESTING THE FUNCTIONALITY OF DFS REPLICATION

1. Open the C:\Replication folder on the W2K8*xx* computer. Create a blank text file called TestReplication.txt.

2. Log off of the odd-numbered computer.

3. Log on to the even-numbered computer as the local administrator.

4. Open the C:\Replication folder on the even-numbered computer. Confirm that the TestReplication.txt file appears.

> **NOTE**
>
> *If the file does not appear immediately, wait a few minutes, and refresh the Windows Explorer screen.*

5. Modify the TestReplication.txt file on the even-numbered computer.

6. Log off of the even-numbered computer.

7. Log on to the odd-numbered computer as the local administrator.

8. Open the C:\Replication\TestReplication.txt file from the odd-numbered computer.

9. Confirm that the changes to the TestReplication.txt file that you made in Step 5 appear.

> **NOTE**
>
> *If the file modifications do not appear immediately, close the file, wait a few minutes, refresh the Windows Explorer screen, and check again.*

10. Log off of the even-numbered computer.

LAB REVIEW QUESTIONS

Completion time	15 minutes

1. In your own words, describe what you learned by completing this lab.

2. When completing Exercise 6.3, where was the configuration information for the \\W2K8*xx*\Public namespace stored?

3. You are configuring DFS-Replication between two offices that share a heavily utilized WAN connection and are concerned that DFS-R replication traffic will overwhelm the link. What feature of DFS-R in Windows Server 2008 can help to minimize the impact of replication over a WAN link?

4. What mechanism will be used by the Public namespace to provide DFS referrals outside of a client's site? What other mechanisms are available?

LAB CHALLENGE 6-1: CONFIGURING A FILE SCREEN

Completion time	15 minutes

Lucerne Publishing management has expressed a concern that users will take up too much room on the new file servers by storing personal files, such as MP3 music files. You want to test the file screen functionality in the File Server Resource Manager to determine whether this can help prevent the issue from occurring.

After completing this exercise, you will know how to:

▲ Configure a file screen in Windows Server 2008

Precautions: If you do not complete the Lab Challenge exercises, you must still complete the Lab Cleanup steps prior to continuing on to Lab 7.

Configure a file screen on the odd-numbered computer to prevent users from saving files with a .MP3 file extension.

NOTE	*You can test the functionality of this File Screen by creating a text file and manually assigning it a ".mp3" file extension.*

LAB CHALLENGE 6-2: CONFIGURING FILE SHARES ON A SERVER CORE COMPUTER

Completion time	15 minutes

To increase the security of servers deployed in several additional remote offices, you have prepared servers running the Windows Server 2008 Server Core installation option to provide infrastructure services to these offices. You must now prepare one of these servers to function as a file server.

After completing this exercise, you will know how to:

▲ Configure file shares from the Windows command line

Precautions: If you do not complete the Lab Challenge exercises, you must still complete the Lab Cleanup steps prior to continuing on to Lab 7.

Log on to the CORE*xx* computer. Create and configure local user accounts and file shares from the Windows command line. (*Hint: key **net /?** at the command prompt to get started.*) Test access to these file shares from a remote computer to confirm the functionality of these shares.

LAB CLEANUP

Completion time	15 minutes

You have completed testing of the File Services server role and now need to reset your Windows Server 2008 computers to their original state prior to performing testing of additional infrastructure services that you are planning to deploy to your production network.

After completing this exercise, you will know how to:

▲ Remove the File Services server role

■ PART A: DELETING THE DFS NAMESPACE AND DFS REPLICATION GROUP ON W2K8*XX*

1. Log on to the W2K8*xx* computer as the administrator of lucernepublishing.com.

2. Click Start→Administrative Tools→DFS Management.

3. Expand Namespaces in the left-hand pane.

4. Right-click W2K8*xx*\Public, and click Delete.

5.   The Confirm Delete Namespace screen appears. Select the Yes, delete the namespace and all its folders radio button, and click OK.

6.   Click Replication in the left-hand pane.

7.   Right-click DFSReplication, and click Delete.

8.   The Confirm Delete Replication Group screen appears. Select the Yes, delete the replication group, stop replicating all associated replicated folders, and delete all members of the replication group, and click OK.

■ PART B: DELETING ALL SHARED FILES AND FOLDERS ON W2K8ZZ AND COREXX

1.   Using Windows Explorer, un-share and delete all shared folders that you have configured on the odd- and even-numbered computers.

> **NOTE** *You may need to reboot both computers after removing the DFS Namespace and DFS Replication group before you will be able to delete the files and folders.*

2.   Delete the C:\DFSRoots folder from the odd-numbered computer.

3.   Using the Computer Management MMC snap-in, delete any local users and groups that you have created on the W2K8*zz* computer.

4.   Using the Windows command-line, un-share and delete all shared folders, users, and groups that you have configured on the CORE*xx* Server Core computer.

■ PART C: REMOVING THE FILE SERVICES SERVER ROLE FROM W2K8ZZ

1.   Log on to the W2K8*zz* server. If the Server Manager console does not appear automatically, click the Start button, and then click Server Manager.

2.   In the left-hand pane of Server Manager, click Roles. In the right-hand pane, click Remove Roles. Click Next.

3.   The Remove Server Roles screen appears. Remove the checkmark next to File Services, and then click Next.

4.   Click Remove, and then click Close when the removal has completed.

5.   When prompted, reboot the W2K8*xx* computer.

6. Log on to the W2K8*zz* server after it reboots. The Server Manager console will reappear automatically. Click Finish when prompted.

7. Log off of the W2K8*zz* server.

■ PART D: DISJOINING THE W2K8ZZ COMPUTER FROM THE LUCERNEPUBLISHING.COM DOMAIN

1. Log on to the W2K8*zz* computer. If Server Manager does not appear automatically, click the Start button, and then click Server Manager.

2. In the right-hand pane of Server Manager, click Change System Properties.

3. The System Properties screen appears. On the Computer Name tab, click Change. In the Member of: section, click the Workgroup radio button, and enter **WORKGROUP** as the workgroup name.

4. Click OK three times, followed by Close.

5. Reboot the computer when prompted.

LAB 7
CONFIGURING PRINT SERVICES

This lab contains the following exercises and activities:

Exercise 7.1	Installing the Print Server Role
Exercise 7.2	Creating and Managing Windows Printers
Exercise 7.3	Installing the Internet Printing Protocol
Lab Review	Questions
Lab Challenge	Publishing Printers in Active Directory Using Group Policy
Lab Cleanup	

BEFORE YOU BEGIN

Lab 7 assumes that setup has been completed as specified in the setup document and that your computer has connectivity to other lab computers and the Internet. The required exercises in Lab 7 assume that you have completed the preparatory exercises in Labs 1 and 2.

The instructor PC is preconfigured as a domain controller in the lucernepublishing.com domain for demonstration purposes and is named INSTRUCTOR01.

> NOTE
>
> *In this lab manual, you will see the characters xx, yy, and zz. These directions assume that you are working on computers configured in pairs and that each computer has a number. One number is odd, and the other number is even. For example, W2K801 is the odd-numbered computer, and W2K802 is the even-numbered computer. When you see xx, substitute the unique number assigned to the odd-numbered computer. When you see yy, substitute the unique number assigned to the even-numbered computer. When you see zz, substitute the number assigned to the computer that you are working at, either odd or even.*

The four Windows Server 2008 server computers referenced in this lab will each be configured with static IP addresses. For ease of reference, record the static IP addresses of each server that you will be working with in this lab:

INSTRUCTOR01 (Instructor Computer)

IP Address: ___.___.___.___

Subnet Mask: ___.___.___.___

Default Gateway: ___.___.___.___

W2K8*xx*: (For example: W2K801)

IP Address: ___.___.___.___

Subnet Mask: ___.___.___.___

Default Gateway: ___.___.___.___

W2K8*yy*: (For example: W2K802)

IP Address: ___.___.___.___

Subnet Mask: ___.___.___.___

Default Gateway: ___.___.___.___

CORE*xx*: (For example: CORE01)

IP Address: ___.___.___.___

Subnet Mask: ___.___.___.___

Default Gateway: ___.___.___.___

SCENARIO

You are a network administrator for Lucerne Publishing. Recently, Lucerne Publishing has opened a new office in an adjacent building that has been connected to the existing Lucerne Publishing network. Now that network connectivity has been established and file sharing capabilities have been tested and deployed, the staff in the new office will require the ability to print documents to local and network-attached printers.

After completing this lab, you will be able to:

- Install the Print Server Role

- Create and manage Windows printers

- Install the Internet Printing Protocol

Estimated lab time: 130 minutes

Exercise 7.1	Installing the Print Server Role
Overview	You have just procured multiple servers to act as print servers within your organization. You must prepare these servers to host the Print Server Role within your organization.
Outcomes	After completing this exercise, you will know how to: ▲ Install the Print Server role
Completion time	20 minutes
Precautions	If working in pairs, this exercise can be performed on both the odd-numbered W2K8*xx* computer and the even-numbered W2K8*yy* computer. If working alone, this exercise can be performed on the odd-numbered W2K8*xx* computer only.

1. Press Ctrl+Alt+Delete on the W2K8*zz* Windows Server 2008 computer assigned to you, and log on as the default administrator of the local computer. Your username will be Administrator. The password will be MSPress#1 or the password that your instructor or lab proctor assigns to you.

2. If the Initial Configuration Tasks (ICT) screen window opens automatically, place a checkmark next to Do not show this window at logon, and click Close.

3. If the Server Manager window does not appear automatically, click the Start button, and then click Server Manager.

4. In the left-hand pane of Server Manager, double-click Roles.

5. Click Add Roles. Click Next to dismiss the initial Welcome screen.

6. The Select Server Roles screen appears. Place a checkmark next to Print Services. Click Next twice to continue.

7. The Select Role Services screen appears. Confirm that there is a checkmark next to Print Server.

8. Click Next, and then click Install. When the Print Services role installation finishes, click Close.

9. Log off of the W2K8*zz* computer.

Exercise 7.2	Creating and Managing Windows Printers
Overview	You have configured two new Windows Server 2008 computers to act as print servers for the new Lucerne Publishing office. You will now configure multiple printers and printer drivers to test the functionality of Windows Server 2008 Print Services.
Outcomes	After completing this exercise, you will know how to: ▲ Install printer drivers ▲ Install printers
Completion time	25 minutes
Precautions	This exercise will be completed using both the even- and odd-numbered computers.

■ PART A: MANAGING PRINTER DRIVERS

1. Log on to the W2K8*zz* computer. Click the Start button, followed by Administrative Tools, followed by Print Management.

2. Drill down to Print Servers→W2K8*zz* (local).

3. Right-click Drivers, and click Add Driver….

4. The Add Printer Driver Wizard screen appears. Click Next.

5. The Processor and Operating System Selection screen appears.

Question 1	*What processor types are listed?*

Question 2	*What processor type(s) are selected by default?*

6. Click Next. The Printer Driver Selection screen appears.

7. In the Manufacturer column, click HP. In the Printers column, click HP LaserJet 4.

8. Click Next, and then clickFinish.

■ PART B: ADDING A LOCAL PRINTER

1. Right-click Printers, and click Add Printer....

2. The Printer Installation screen appears.

Question 3	*What installation methods are available?*

3. Select the Add a new printer using an existing port radio button. Select LPT1: (Printer Port) in the drop-down box.

4. Click Next. The Printer Driver screen appears.

5. Click the Use an existing printer driver on the computer radio button. Select HP LaserJet 4 in the drop-down box.

6. Click Next. The Printer Name and Sharing Settings screen appears.

7. Accept the default settings.

8. Click Next twice, followed by Finish.

■ PART C: CREATING A PRINTER POOL

1. Right-click Printers, and click Add Printer....

2. The Printer Installation screen appears.

3. Select the Add a new printer using an existing port radio button. Select LPT2: (Printer Port) in the drop-down box.

4. Click Next. The Printer Driver screen appears.

5. Click the Use an existing printer driver on the computer radio button. Select HP LaserJet 4 in the drop-down box.

6. Click Next. The Printer Name and Sharing Settings screen appears.

7. Accept the default settings.

8. Click Next twice, and then click Finish.

9. Double-click Printers in the left-hand pane. Right-click HP LaserJet 4, and select Properties.

10. Select the Ports tab. Place a checkmark next to Enable Printer Pooling.

11. Place a checkmark next to LPT2:, and click OK.

■ PART D: CONFIRMING PRINTER SECURITY SETTINGS.

1. Double-click Printers in the left-hand pane. Right-click HP LaserJet 4, and click Properties.

2. Select the Security tab.

Question 4	*What are the default security settings for the printer?*

■ PART E: CUSTOMIZING PRINTER SETTINGS

1. Select the Advanced tab.

2. Select the Available from: radio button, and set the printer schedule so that it is available from 8am to 5pm.

Question 5	*What is the printer's default priority?*

3. Click Cancel. Log off of the W2K8*zz* computer.

Exercise 7.3	Installing the Internet Printing Protocol
Overview	The Lucerne Publishing IT department has decided to test the functionality of Web-based printing in Windows Server 2008 for the newly opened office. You need to install the Internet Printing Protocol (IPP) on two Windows Server 2008 computers that you are using to test print server functionality.
Outcomes	After completing this exercise, you will know how to: ▲ Install and configure the Internet Printing Protocol (IPP)
Completion time	25 minutes
Precautions	If students are working in pairs, this exercise will be completed using both the even- and odd-numbered computers. If students are working alone, this exercise can be performed on the odd-numbered W2K8*xx* computer only.

■ PART A: DISABLING ENHANCED INTERNET SECURITY

1. Press Ctrl+Alt+Delete on the W2K8*zz* computer assigned to you, and log on as the default administrator of the local computer. Your username will be Administrator. The password will be MSPress#1 or the password that your instructor or lab proctor assigns to you.

2. Click Start→Server Manager. In the right-hand pane, scroll to the Security Information section. Click Configure IE ESC.

3. The Internet Explorer Enhanced Security Configuration window appears. In the Administrators section, select the Off radio button, and click OK.

■ PART B: INSTALLING THE INTERNET PRINTING PROTOCOL

1. Click Start→Server Manager. Click the plus sign (+) next to Roles.

2. Right-click Print Services, and click Add Role Services.

3. The Select Role Services screen appears. Place a checkmark next to Internet Printing.

4. The Add Role Services screen appears.

Question 6	What roles must be added to enable Internet Printing?

5. Click Add Required Role Services.

6. Click Next three times, and then click Install.

7. When the installation completes, click Close.

■ PART C: CONFIRMING THE FUNCTIONALITY OF INTERNET PRINTING ON THE LOCAL COMPUTER

1. Click the Start button. Key **http://w2k8zz/printers**.

2. The Connect to W2K8zz screen appears. Enter the administrator username and password for W2K8zz, and click OK.

3. The Microsoft Phishing Filter screen appears. Click the Turn on Automatic Phishing Filter (recommended) radio button, and click OK.

4. If the Do You See The Information Bar? screen appears, place a checkmark next to Don't show this message again, and click OK.

5. If the Information Bar reads "Intranet settings are now turned off by default. Intranet settings are less secure than Internet settings. Click here for more options…," click the Information Bar, and select Enable Intranet Settings. Click Yes to confirm.

Question 7	What is the name of the Web page that is displayed?

6. Click HP Laserjet 4.

Question 8	What commands are listed in the left-hand column?

LAB REVIEW QUESTIONS

Completion time	15 minutes

1. In your own words, describe what you learned by completing this lab.

2. What is the difference between the Manage Printers permission and the Manage Documents permission?

3. What is the difference between EMF, PCL, and XPS?

LAB CHALLENGE: PUBLISHING PRINTERS IN ACTIVE DIRECTORY USING GROUP POLICY

Completion time	30 minutes

Once you have completed testing of the Windows Server 2008 print server functionality, you wish to start deploying printers automatically via Group Policy Objects within the Lucerne Publishing Active Directory domain.

After completing this exercise, you will know how to:

▲ Deploy printers via Group Policy

Working with your instructor, join the W2K8*zz* and VISTA*xx* computers to the Lucerne Publishing Active Directory domain. Create a Group Policy Object that will deploy the HP LaserJet 4 printer to the Domain Users group in Active Directory.

> **NOTE**
>
> *Your instructor has already created one or more test user accounts in a test Organizational Unit (OU) and has created a sample GPO to help you test this functionality.*

LAB CLEANUP

Completion time	15 minutes

You have completed testing of the Print Services server role and now need to reset your Windows Server 2008 computers to their original state prior to performing testing of additional infrastructure services that you are planning to deploy to your production network.

After completing this exercise, you will know how to:

▲ Remove the Print Services server role

■ PART A: DELETING SHARED PRINTERS FROM W2K8ZZ

1. Log on to the W2K8*zz* computer as the administrator of lucernepublishing.com.

2. Click Start→Administrative Tools→Print Management.

3. Expand Print Servers→W2K8*zz* (local)→Printers in the left-hand pane.

4. Right-click HP LaserJet 4, and click Delete. Click Yes to confirm.

5. Right-click HP LaserJet 4 (Copy 1), and click Delete. Click Yes to confirm.

6. Close the Print Management Console.

■ PART B: REMOVING THE PRINT SERVICES ROLE

1. Click the Start button, and then click Server Manager.

2. Click the plus sign next to Roles. Right-click Roles, and then click Remove Roles.

3. Click Next. The Remove Server Roles screen appears.

4. Remove the checkmark next to Print Services and Web Server (IIS).

5. Click Next. Confirm that the Delete printers installed on the server radio button is selected.

6. Click Next, and then click Remove.

7. Click Close, and then click Yes to reboot the server.

8. When the computer reboots, log on as the administrator of the lucernepublishing.com domain. Click Close when the Remove Roles Wizard appears.

9. Log off of the W2K8*zz* computer.

■ PART C (IF LAB CHALLENGE WAS COMPLETED): DISJOINING THE W2K8ZZ COMPUTER FROM THE LUCERNEPUBLISHING.COM DOMAIN

1. Log on to the W2K8*zz* computer. If Server Manager does not appear automatically, click the Start button, and then click Server Manager.

2. In the right-hand pane of Server Manager, click Change System Properties.

3. The System Properties screen appears. On the Computer Name tab, click Change. In the Member of: section, click the Workgroup radio button, and enter **WORKGROUP** as the workgroup name.

4. Click OK three times, followed by Close.

5. Reboot the computer when prompted.

LAB 8
MAINTAINING AND UPDATING WINDOWS SERVER 2008

This lab contains the following exercises and activities:

Exercise 8.1	Using the Reliability and Performance Monitor
Exercise 8.2	Using the Windows Event Viewer
Exercise 8.3	Installing and Using the Windows Network Monitor
Exercise 8.4	Installing and Configuring WSUS
Lab Review	Questions
Lab Challenge	Creating a Computer Group in WSUS
Lab Cleanup	

BEFORE YOU BEGIN

Lab 8 assumes that setup has been completed as specified in the setup document and that your computer has connectivity to other lab computers and the Internet. The required exercises in Lab 8 assumes that you have completed the preparatory exercises in Labs 1 and 2.

The instructor PC is preconfigured as a domain controller in the lucernepublishing.com domain for demonstration purposes, and it is named INSTRUCTOR01. Before completing Exercise 8.3, configure each computer to use the INSTRUCTOR01 computer as its preferred DNS server as described in Lab 1 and Lab 2.

> **NOTE**
>
> *In this lab manual, you will see the characters xx, yy, and zz. These directions assume that you are working on computers configured in pairs and that each computer has a number. One number is odd, and the other number is even. For example, W2K801 is the odd-numbered computer, and W2K802 is the even-numbered computer. When you see xx, substitute the unique number assigned to the odd-numbered computer. When you see yy, substitute the unique number assigned to the even-numbered computer. When you see zz, substitute the number assigned to the computer that you are working at, either odd or even.*

The four Windows Server 2008 server computers referenced in this lab will each be configured with static IP addresses. For ease of reference, record the static IP addresses of each server that you will be working with in this lab:

INSTRUCTOR01 (Instructor Computer)

IP Address: ___.___.___.___

Subnet Mask: ___.___.___.___

Default Gateway: ___.___.___.___

W2K8*xx*: (For example: W2K801)

IP Address: ___.___.___.___

Subnet Mask: ___.___.___.___

Default Gateway: ___.___.___.___

W2K8*yy*: (For example: W2K802)

IP Address: ___.___.___.___

Subnet Mask: ___.___.___.___

Default Gateway: ___.___.___.___

CORE*xx*: (For example: CORE01)

IP Address: ___.___.___.___

Subnet Mask: ___.___.___.___

Default Gateway: ___.___.___.___

SCENARIO

You are a network administrator for Lucerne Publishing. Lucerne Publishing is in the process of deploying numerous Windows Server 2008 computers to several remote locations in order to provide infrasturcture services such as DHCP, DNS, and File and Print Services. In order to make provisions for future purchase decisions as well as maintaining ongoing operational efficiency, you now need to put a plan in place to monitor the performance of the Lucerne Publishing servers and network connectivity. Additionally, you wish to deploy a centralized solution to deploy security patches and updates to the Lucerne Publishing servers.

After completing this lab, you will be able to:

■ Use the Reliability and Performance Monitor

■ Use the Windows Event Viewer

■ Install and use the Windows Network Monitor

■ Install and configure WSUS

Estimated lab time: 180 minutes

Exercise 8.1	Using the Reliability and Performance Monitor
Overview	You have finished testing multiple servers to act as infrastructure servers within your organization. You will now test the Reliability and Performance Monitor functionality within Windows Server 2008.
Outcomes	After completing this exercise, you will know how to: ▲ Launch the Reliability and Performance Monitor ▲ Add counters to Performance Monitor ▲ View reports in Reliability Monitor
Completion time	20 minutes
Precautions	If students are working in pairs, this exercise should be performed on both the odd-numbered W2K8*xx* computer and the even-numbered W2K8*yy* computer. If students are working alone, this exercise can be performed on the odd-numbered W2K8*xx* computer only.

1. Press Ctrl+Alt+Delete on the W2K8*zz* Windows Server 2008 computer assigned to you, and log on as the default administrator of the local computer. Your username will be Administrator. The password will be MSPress#1 or the password that your instructor or lab proctor assigns to you.

2. If the Initial Configuration Tasks (ICT) screen window opens automatically, place a checkmark next to Do not show this window at logon, and click Close.

3. If the Server Manager window does not appear automatically, click the Start button, and then click Server Manager.

4. In the left-hand pane of Server Manager, expand Diagnostics.

5. Expand Reliability and Performance, and then expand Monitoring Tools.

Question 1	What headings are available in the right-hand pane?

6. Click Performance Monitor in the left-hand pane.

7. Click the green plus-sign toolbar button in the middle pane. The Add Counters screen appears.

8. Click the plus sign next to Processor in the Available Counters section. In the lower left-hand corner of the Add Counters screen, place a checkmark next to Show description.

9. Click % Idle Time.

Question 2	What is monitored by % Idle time?

Question 3	What instances are available in the Instances of selected object section?

10. Click Total, and then click Add. Click OK.

11. Click the % Idle Time line in the legend underneath the graph.

Question 4	What is the average value of % Idle Time on the W2K8zz computer?

12. Click the green plus sign in the middle pane. The Add Counters screen appears.

13. Click the plus sign next to System in the Available Counters section.

14. Click Processor Queue Length, and then click Add.

15. Click OK. Click the Processor Queue Length line in the middle pane.

Question 5	What is the average value of Processor Queue Length on the W2K8zz computer?

16. Click Reliability Monitor in the left-hand pane.

Question 6	What subheadings are available in the System Stability Report section?

17. Close Server Manager. Log off of the W2K8zz computer.

Exercise 8.2   Using the Windows Event Viewer

Overview	You have finished testing multiple servers to act as infrastructure servers within your organization. You will now test the Windows Event Viewer functionality within Windows Server 2008.
Outcomes	After completing this exercise, you will know how to: ▲ Launch the Windows Event Viewer ▲ Create a Custom Event Log view
Completion time	25 minutes
Precautions	If students are working in pairs, this exercise should be performed on both the odd-numbered W2K8xx computer and the even-numbered W2K8yy computer. If students are working alone, this exercise can be performed on the odd-numbered W2K8xx computer only.

■ **PART A: WORKING WITH THE WINDOWS EVENT VIEWER**

1. Log on to the W2K8zz computer. Click the Start button, followed by Server Manager.

2. Drill down to Diagnostics→Windows Event Viewer.

3. Expand Windows Logs.

> **Question 7**
>
> *What logs are available by default?*

4. Click Application in the left pane.

> **Question 8**
>
> *What is the most recent Event ID logged to the Application log?*

5. Click Security in the left pane.

> **Question 9**
>
> *What is the most recent Event ID logged to the Security log?*

6. Click Setup in the left pane.

> **Question 10**
>
> *What is the most recent Event ID logged to the Setup log?*

7. Click System in the left pane.

> **Question 11**
>
> *What is the most recent Event ID logged to the System log?*

■ PART B: CREATING A CUSTOM EVENT VIEWER VIEW

1. In the left-hand pane, drill down to Diagnostics→Event Viewer→Custom Views.

2. Right-click Custom Views, and click Create Custom View…. The Create Custom View screen appears.

3. In the Event level: section, place a checkmark next to Critical and Warning.

4. In the Event logs: drop-down box, expand Windows Logs, and then place a checkmark next to Application and System.

5. Click OK. The Save Filter to Custom View screen appears.

6. In the Name field, enter **Critical and Warning Events Only**. Click OK.

Question 12	*How many events are displayed in this Custom View?*

7. Close Server Manager. Log off of the W2K8*zz* computer.

Exercise 8.3	Installing and Using the Windows Network Monitor
Overview	You have finished testing multiple servers to act as infrastructure servers within your organization. You will now test Windows Network Monitor to allow you to monitor and troubleshoot network traffic in Windows Server 2008.
Outcomes	After completing this exercise, you will know how to: ▲ Install and configure Windows Network Monitor ▲ Perform a network capture ▲ Create a Capture Filter
Completion time	30 minutes
Precautions	This exercise will be completed using both the even- and odd-numbered computers. The required installers will be available from a shared folder on the \\INSTRUCTOR01\ computer, or they can be downloaded from the Microsoft Web site.

■ PART A: INSTALLING NETWORK MONITOR

1. Press Ctrl+Alt+Delete on the W2K8*zz* computer assigned to you, and log on as the default administrator of the local computer. Your username will be Administrator. The password will be MSPress#1 or the password that your instructor or lab proctor assigns to you.

2. Copy the installation file for Network Monitor from the \\INSTRUCTOR01\ computer to the root of the C:\ drive on W2K8*zz*. Double-click the file, and then click Run.

3. The Welcome to the Microsoft Network Monitor 3.1 Setup Wizard screen appears. Click Next.

4. The End-User License Agreement screen appears. Select the I accept the terms in the License Agreement radio button. Click Next.

5. The Use Microsoft Update to Help Keep your Computer Secure and Up to Date screen appears. Click the Use Microsoft Update when I check for updates (recommended) radio button. Click Next.

6. The Customer Experience Improvement Program screen appears. Select the I do not want to participate in the program at this time radio button. Click Next.

7. The Choose Setup Type screen appears. Click Complete.

8. The Ready to Install screen appears. Click Install.

NOTE	*If your lab environment does not allow Internet access, you may receive an error message about Microsoft Update. Click OK to continue if this happens.*

9. Click Finish when the installation completes.

■ PART B: USING NETWORK MONITOR TO VIEW NETWORK TRAFFIC

1. Double-click the Network Monitor 3.1 shortcut that now appears on the W2K8*zz* desktop. If this is the first time you've opened Network Monitor 3.1, the Microsoft Update Opt-In screen will appear. Click No.

2. The Microsoft Network Monitor 3.1 screen appears. Place a checkmark next to Enable conversations (consumes more memory). Click Create a new capture tab....

3. Click Capture→Start to begin a network capture. To simulate network traffic, open a command prompt, and perform an nslookup of the W2K8*xx* and W2K8*yy* computers. Close the command prompt window.

Question 13	*What is the keyboard shortcut to begin a network capture?*

4. After the capture runs for a minute, click Capture→Stop to stop the network capture.

5. In the Network Conversations pane, double-click My Traffic, and then double-click IPv4.

■ PART C: CREATING A CAPTURE FILTER

1. Click File→New→Capture. Click Filter→Capture Filter→Load Filter→Standard Filters→DNS.

Question 14	What appears in the Capture Filter pane?

2. Click Apply in the Capture Filter pane.

3. Press F10 to begin a new capture.

Question 15	Does anything appear in the Network Conversations pane? Why or why not?

4. Open a command prompt window. Key **nslookup <Name of your partner's computer>**, and press Enter.

Question 16	Does anything appear in the Network Conversations pane? Why or why not?

5. Close Network Monitor. Log off of the W2K8*zz* computer.

Exercise 8.4	Installing and Configuring WSUS
Overview	You have finished testing multiple servers to act as infrastructure servers within your organization. You now want to test Windows Server Update Services as a means of providing automated security updates to these servers.
Outcomes	After completing this exercise, you will know how to: ▲ Install and configure Windows Server Update Services ▲ Administer Windows Server Update Services ▲ Configure Windows Server Update Services client settings
Completion time	45 minutes
Precautions	Part A and B of this exercise will be completed from the odd-numbered computer. The required installers will be available on the \\INSTRUCTOR01 computer, or else they can be downloaded from the Microsoft Web site. If the lab computers do not have Internet access, the lab instructor or proctor will provide alternate configuration instructions to configure the WSUS server in Part C. If the lab computers require a proxy server to access the Internet, the lab instructor or proctor will provide the necessary configuration instructions in Part C.

■ PART A: INSTALLING WSUS PREREQUISITES ON THE ODD-NUMBERED COMPUTER

1. Press Ctrl+Alt+Delete on the W2K8*xx* computer assigned to you, and log on as the default administrator of the local computer. Your username will be Administrator. The password will be MSPress#1 or the password that your instructor or lab proctor assigns to you.

2. If the Server Manager screen does not appear automatically, click Start→Server Manager.

3. Click Roles→Add Roles. The Before You Begin screen begins. Click Next.

4. The Select Server Roles screen appears. Place a checkmark next to Web Server (IIS). (If prompted, click Add Required Role Services.)

5. Click Next twice. The Select Role Services screen appears. Place a checkmark next to the following optional components (again, if prompted, click Add Required Role Services):

    - ASP.NET

    - Windows Authentication

    - IIS 6 Management Compatibility

6. Click Next, followed by Install.

7. Click Close when the installation completes.

8. Copy the Microsoft Report Viewer installer from the \\INSTRUCTOR01\ computer to the root of the C:\ drive.

9. Open the C:\ drive in Windows Explorer. Double-click the Microsoft Report Viewer installer. Click Run to open the file.

10. The Welcome to Microsoft Report Viewer Redistributable 2005 Setup screen appears. Click Next.

11. The End-User License Agreement screen appears. Place a checkmark next to I accept the terms of the License Agreement, and click Install. Click Finish when the installation completes.

12. Log off of the W2K8*xx* computer.

■ PART B: INSTALLING WSUS 3.0 SERVICE PACK 1 ON THE ODD-NUMBERED COMPUTER

1. Press Ctrl+Alt+Delete on the W2K8*xx* computer assigned to you, and log on as the default administrator of the local computer. Your username will be Administrator. The password will be MSPress#1 or the password that your instructor or lab proctor assigns to you.

2. Copy the WSUS 3.0 SP1 installer from the \\INSTRUCTOR01\shared folder to the root of the C:\ drive.

3. Double-click the WSUS 3.0 SP1 installer. If prompted, click Run to open the file.

4. Click Next. The Installation Mode Selection screen appears. Ensure that the Full server installation including Administration Console radio button is selected, and click Next.

5. The License Agreement screen appears. Select the I Accept the terms of the License Agreement radio button, and click Next.

6. The Select Update Source screen appears. Accept the default value, and click Next.

Question 17	Where will WSUS downloads be stored by default?

7. The Database Options screen appears. Accept the default selection, and click Next.

Question 18	What database does WSUS use by default?

8. The Web Site Selection screen appears. Accept the default selection, and click Next.

9. Click Next to begin. The installation will take several minutes to complete. Click Finish when prompted.

10. Remain logged on to the W2K8*xx* computer to perform the next section.

■ PART C: PERFORMING THE INITIAL CONFIGURATION OF WSUS

1. After a short pause, the Windows Server Update Services Configuration Wizard appears. On the Before you Begin screen, click Next.

2. The Join the Microsoft Update Improvement Program screen appears. Remove the checkmark next to Yes, I would like to join the Microsoft Update Improvement Program, and then click Next.

3. The Choose Upstream Server screen appears. Ensure that the Synchronize from Microsoft Update radio button is selected, and click Next.

NOTE	*If your lab environment does not have Internet access, your lab instructor or proctor will instruct you to select the Synchronize from another Windows Server Update Services server radio button and will provide the necessary configuration information.*

4. The Specify Proxy Server screen appears. Accept the default selections, and click Next.

> **NOTE**
>
> *If your lab environment requires proxy server configuration, your lab instructor or proctor will instruct you to place a checkmark next to Use a proxy server when synchronizing and will provide the necessary configuration information.*

5. The Connect to Upstream Server screen appears. Click Start Connecting.

> **NOTE**
>
> *Establishing a connection to the Windows Update site may take several minutes before the next screen appears.*

6. Click Next. The Choose Languages screen appears. Accept the default selection, and click Next.

> **NOTE**
>
> *If appropriate, remove the checkmark next to English, and select the language(s) applicable to your lab environment.*

7. The Choose Products screen appears. To save disk space on the lab computers, remove the checkmark next to Office and Windows. Place a checkmark next to Windows Server 2008 and Windows Vista.

8. Click Next. The Choose Classifications screen appears. Accept the default selections, and click Next.

> **Question 19**
>
> *What types of updates does WSUS download by default?*

9. Click Next. The Set Sync Schedule screen appears. Ensure that the Synchronize manually radio button is selected, and then click Next.

10. The Finished screen appears. Remove the checkmark next to Begin initial synchronization, and click Next.

11. The What's Next screen appears. Click Finish to exit the wizard.

12. Remain logged on to the W2K8*xx* computer for the next section.

■ PART D: ADMINISTERING A WSUS SERVER

1. If the Update Services MMC does not appear automatically, click Start→Administrative Tools→Microsoft Windows Server Update Services 3.0 SP1. Expand the W2K8*xx* node.

Question 20	*What nodes are available under the W2K8xx node?*

2. Click Synchronizations. Right-click Synchronizations, and click Synchronize Now. In the main MMC panel, the status of the Synchronization will change from Running… to Succeeded.

3. When the synchronization completes, click Options. Click Products and Classifications.

4. In the Products tab, place a checkmark next to Windows Server 2003. Click OK.

5. Log off of the W2K8*xx* computer.

■ PART E: CONFIGURING THE EVEN-NUMBERED COMPUTER TO RECEIVE UPDATES FROM WSUS

1. Log on to the W2K8*yy* computer as Administrator.

2. Open a command prompt. Confirm that you can successfully ping the W2K8*xx* computer. Close the command prompt window.

3. Click Start, key **gpedit.msc,** and click Enter.

4. The Local Group Policy Editor window appears. Browse to Computer Configuration→Administrative Templates→Windows Components→Windows Update.

5. In the right-hand pane, double-click Configure Automatic Updates.

6. The Configure Automatic Updates Properties screen appears. Select the Enabled radio button. Click OK.

7. In the right-hand pane, double-click Specify intranet Microsoft update service location.

8. The Specify Intranet Microsoft Update Service Location Properties window appears. Select Enabled. In the Set the intranet update service for detecting updates text box, enter **http://w2k8xx**. In the Set the intranet statistics server text box, enter **http://W2K8xx**. Click OK.

9. Click Start→Administrative Tools→Services. Right-click Windows Update, and click Restart.

10. Open a command prompt. At the command prompt, key **wuauclt/detectnow**, and press Enter. Close the command prompt window.

11. Log off of the W2K8*yy* computer.

■ **PART F: CONFIRMING THE CONFIGURATION OF THE AUTOMATIC UPDATES CLIENT ON THE EVEN-NUMBERED COMPUTER**

1. Log on to the W2K8*xx* computer as the local administrator.

2. Click Start→Administrative Tools→Update Services.

3. Expand W2K8*xx*→Computers→All Computers.

4. In the Status: drop-down box, select Any. Click Refresh.

Question 21	What is the last status reported from the W2K8yy computer?

5. Log off of the W2K8*xx* computer.

LAB REVIEW QUESTIONS

Completion time	15 minutes

1. In your own words, describe what you learned by completing this lab.

2. What are the IIS prerequisites needed to install WSUS 3.0 SP1?

3. What reports are available in the Update Services MMC?

4. What exception must be configured in the Windows Firewall to view Event Viewer on a remote computer?

LAB CHALLENGE: CREATING A COMPUTER GROUP IN WSUS

Completion time	30 minutes

Once you have completed testing of WSUS, you want to configure the ability to specify different lists of approved updates for different groups of computers on the Lucerne Publishing network.

After completing this exercise, you will know how to:

▲ Create a computer group in WSUS

▲ Configure a Windows Vista computer for WSUS

Precautions: If you do not complete the Lab Challenge exercises, you must still complete the Lab Cleanup steps prior to continuing on to Lab 9.

Create a computer group in the Update Services MMC called AllVista. Configure the VISTA*xx* computer to use W2K8*xx* for updates, and configure it to be a part of the AllVista targeted group.

LAB CLEANUP

Completion time	15 minutes

You have completed testing of Windows updating and monitoring functions and now need to reset your Windows Server 2008 computers to their original state prior to performing testing of additional infrastructure services that you are planning to deploy to your production network.

After completing this exercise, you will know how to:

▲ Remove the IIS Server role

▲ Uninstall software from a Windows Server 2008 computer

▲ Remove Local Group Policy Object configuration items

■ PART A: UNINSTALLING SOFTWARE FROM THE W2K8ZZ COMPUTER

1. Log on to the W2K8*zz* computer as the local administrator.

2. Click Start→Control Panel.

3. Double-click Programs and Features.

4. The Programs and Features window appears. Right-click Microsoft Network Monitor, and click Uninstall/Change.

5. Follow the prompts to uninstall the Microsoft Network Monitor.

6. Delete all installation files that you copied to the W2K8*zz* computer from the INSTRUCTOR01 computer.

7. Remove the INSTRUCTOR01 server as the W2K8*zz* computer's preferred DNS server.

8. Log off of the W2K8*zz* computer.

■ PART B: UNINSTALLING REMAINING SOFTWARE FROM THE W2K8*XX* COMPUTER

1. Log on to the W2K8*xx* computer as the local administrator.

2. Click Start→Control Panel.

3. Double-click Programs and Features.

4. The Programs and Features window appears. Right-click Microsoft Report Viewer Redistributable 2005, and click Uninstall/Change.

5. Follow the prompts to uninstall the Microsoft Report Viewer Redistributable 2005.

6. Right-click Microsoft Windows Server Update Services 3.0 SP1, and click Uninstall/Change.

7. Follow the prompts to uninstall all components of Microsoft Windows Server Update Services 3.0 SP1.

8. Click Start→Server Manager. Click Features, and then click Remove Features. Follow the prompts to uninstall the following features:

   - Windows Internal Database

   - Windows Process Activation Database (when prompted, click Remove Dependent Role Services)

9. Restart the computer when prompted.

10. After the server restarts, log on as the local administrator. Return to the Server Manager console. Click Roles, and then click Remove Roles. Follow the prompts to uninstall the Web Server (IIS) role.

11. Restart the computer when prompted.

■ PART C: REMOVING WSUS CONFIGURATION ON W2K8*YY*

1. Log on to the W2K8*yy* computer as the local administrator. Click Start, then key **gpedit.msc**, and click Enter.

2. Browse to Computer Configuration→Administrative Templates→Windows Components→Windows Update.

3. In the right-hand pane, double-click Configure Automatic Updates.

4. The Configure Automatic Updates Properties screen appears. Select the Not Configured radio button. Click OK.

5. In the right-hand pane, double-click Specify intranet Microsoft update service location.

6. The Specify Intranet Microsoft Update Service Location Properties window appears. Select the Not Configured radio button. Click OK.

7. Log off of the W2K8*yy* computer.

LAB 9
SECURING DATA TRANSMISSION AND AUTHENTICATION

This lab contains the following exercises and activities:

Exercise 9.1   Configuring IPSec to Allow and Block Traffic

Exercise 9.2   Managing IPSec Authentication and Encryption Settings

Exercise 9.3   Configuring the Windows Firewall

Exercise 9.4   Configuring Connection Security Rules

Exercise 9.5   Configuring the Windows Firewall on Server Core (optional)

Lab Review   Questions

Lab Challenge   Configuring the Remote Administration Exception

Lab Cleanup

BEFORE YOU BEGIN

Lab 9 assumes that setup has been completed as specified in the setup document and that your computer has connectivity to other lab computers and the Internet. The required exercises in Lab 9 assume that you have completed the preparatory exercises in Labs 1 and 2.

The instructor PC is preconfigured as a domain controller in the lucernepublishing.com domain for demonstration purposes and is named INSTRUCTOR01.

NOTE	*In this lab manual, you will see the characters xx, yy, and zz. These directions assume that you are working on computers configured in pairs and that each computer has a number. One number is odd, and the other number is even. For example, W2K801 is the odd-numbered computer, and W2K802 is the even-numbered computer. When you see xx, substitute the unique number assigned to the odd-numbered computer. When you see yy, substitute the unique number assigned to the even-numbered computer. When you see zz, substitute the number assigned to the computer that you are working at, either odd or even.*

The four Windows Server 2008 server computers referenced in this lab will each be configured with static IP addresses. For ease of reference, record the static IP addresses of each server that you will be working with in this lab:

INSTRUCTOR01 (Instructor Computer)

IP Address: ___.___.___.___

Subnet Mask: ___.___.___.___

Default Gateway: ___.___.___.___

W2K8*xx*: (For example: W2K801)

IP Address: ___.___.___.___

Subnet Mask: ___.___.___.___

Default Gateway: ___.___.___.___

W2K8*yy*: (For example: W2K802)

IP Address: ___.___.___.___

Subnet Mask: ___.___.___.___

Default Gateway: ___.___.___.___

CORE*xx*: (For example: CORE01)

IP Address: ___.___.___.___

Subnet Mask: ___.___.___.___

Default Gateway: ___.___.___.___

SCENARIO

You are a network administrator for Lucerne Publishing. Lucerne Publishing is in the process of deploying numerous Windows Server 2008 computers to several remote locations to provide infrastructure services such as DHCP, DNS, and File and Print Services. To address management concerns about maintaining the security of access to these servers, you are investigating the use of IPSec and the Windows Firewall on a Windows Server 2008 network.

After completing this lab, you will be able to:

- Configure IPSec to allow and block traffic

- Manage IPSec authentication and encryption settings

- Configure the Windows Firewall and connection security rules

- (Optional) Configure the Windows Firewall on Server Core

Estimated lab time: 230 minutes

Exercise 9.1	Configuring IPSec to Allow and Block Traffic
Overview	You have finished testing multiple servers to act as file and print servers within your organization. You will now test the ability of IPSec filtering to grant and deny access to these servers from specific ranges of IP addresses.
Outcomes	After completing this exercise, you will know how to: ▲ Manage IPSec filter lists and filter actions ▲ Create and assign a local IPSec Policy
Completion time	30 minutes
Precautions	Part A of this exercise will be completed on both the odd- and even-numbered computers. The remaining portions of the exercise will indicate which computer should be used.

■ PART A: CONFIGURING THE WINDOWS FIREWALL TO ALLOW PING

1. Press Ctrl+Alt+Delete on the W2K8*xx* Windows Server 2008 computer assigned to you, and log on as the default administrator of the local computer. Your username will be Administrator. The password will be MSPress#1 or the password that your instructor or lab proctor assigns to you.

2. Click Start→Administrative Tools→Windows Firewall with Advanced Security.

3. Click Inbound Rules. Right-click Inbound Rules, and click New Rule….

4. The Rule Type screen appears. Click the Custom radio button, and click Next.

5. The Program screen appears. Click the All programs radio button, and click Next.

6. The Protocol and Ports screen appears. In the Protocol type drop-down box, click ICMPv4.

7. Click Next 4 times.

8. The Name screen appears. In the Name: text box, enter **Lab 9 Allow Ping**. Click Finish.

9. Log off of the W2K8*zz* computer.

■ PART B: CONFIGURING IPSEC FILTER ACTIONS ON THE ODD-NUMBERED COMPUTER

1. Press Ctrl+Alt+Delete on the W2K8*xx* Windows Server 2008 computer assigned to you, and log on as the default administrator of the local computer. Your username will be Administrator. The password will be MSPress#1 or the password that your instructor or lab proctor assigns to you.

2. If the Initial Configuration Tasks (ICT) screen window opens automatically, place a checkmark next to Do not show this window at logon, and click Close.

3. Click Start, key **gpedit.msc**, and press Enter.

4. The Local Group Policy Editor window appears. Drill down to Computer Configuration→Windows Settings→Security Settings→IP Security Policies on Local Computer.

5. Right-click IP Security Policies on Local Computer, and click Manage IP filter lists and filter actions.

6. The IP Filter Lists and Filter Actions screen appears. On the Manage IP Filter Lists tab, click Add.

7. The IP Filter List screen appears. In the Name: text box, enter **Lab 9 IP Filter List**.

8. Click Add, and then click Next.

9. The IP Filter Description and Mirrored Property screen appears. In the Description: text box, enter **Filter traffic to and from the even-numbered computer**.

10. Click Next. The IP Traffic Source screen appears.

Question 1	What are the available options for Source address?

11. In the Source address: drop-down box, select A Specific IP Address or Subnet. In the IP Address: text box, enter the IP address of the W2K8*yy* even-numbered computer.

12. Click Next. The IP Traffic Destination screen appears. In the Destination IP Address: drop-down box, select My IP Address.

13. Click Next. The IP Protocol Type screen appears. Accept the default selection, and click Next.

Question 2	What is the default protocol type?

14. Click Finish, and then click OK.

15. Leave the Manage IP Filter Lists and Filter Actions screen open for the next section.

■ PART C: CONFIGURING IPSEC BLOCK AND ALLOW ACTIONS

1. Click the Manage Filter Actions tab. Click Add, and then click Next.

2. The Filter Action Name screen appears. In the Name: text box, enter **Block-Traffic**. Click Next.

3. The Filter Action General Options screen appears.

Question 3	What action types are available to choose from?

4. Select the Block radio button, and then click Next. Click Finish.

5. Repeat Steps 1-4 to create a Filter Action called Permit-Traffic with a Filter Action of Permit.

6. Click Close.

7. Remain logged on to the odd-numbered computer for the next section.

■ PART D: CREATING AND ASSIGNING AN IPSEC POLICY

1. Right-click IPSec Security Policies on Local Computer. Click Create IPSec Security Policy…, then click Next.

2. The IPSec Security Policy Name screen appears. In the Name: text box, enter **Lab 9 IPSec Policy**. Click Next twice to continue.

3. Ensure that the Edit Properties checkbox is selected, and then click Finish.

4. The Lab 9 IPSec Policy screen appears. Select the General tab.

Question 4	How often will the local computer check for policy updates?

5. Select the Rules tab. Click Add, and then click Next.

6. The Tunnel Endpoint screen appears. Click Next. The Network Type screen appears.

Question 5	What are the network types to which this rule can be applied?

7. Click Next. The IP Filter List screen appears. Select the radio button next to the Lab 9 IP Filter List that you created in Section A. Click Next.

8. The Filter Action screen appears. Select the radio button next to the Block-Traffic IP Filter Action that you created in Section B. Click Next.

9. Click Finish, and then click OK.

10. Remain logged on to the W2K8*xx* computer.

■ PART E: CONFIRMING THE FUNCTIONALITY OF THE IPSEC POLICY

1. Log on to the even-numbered computer as a local administrator. Open a command prompt.

Question 6	*Are you able to ping the IP address of the odd-numbered computer?*

2. Remain logged on to the even-numbered computer.

3. Return to the odd-numbered computer. Right-click Lab 9 IPSec Policy, and click Assign.

4. Remain logged on to the W2K8*xx* computer.

5. Return to the even-numbered computer as a local administrator.

Question 7	*Are you now able to ping the IP address of the odd-numbered computer?*

6. Return to the odd-numbered computer. Right-click Lab 9 IPSec Policy, and click Un-assign.

7. Return to the even-numbered computer.

Question 8	*Are you now able to ping the IP address of the odd-numbered computer?*

8. Log off of the even-numbered computer.

9. Log off of the odd-numbered computer.

Exercise 9.2	Managing IPSec Authentication and Encryption Settings
Overview	You will now test the ability of IPSec to secure communication between two computers.
Outcomes	After completing this exercise, you will know how to: ▲ Configure IPSec encryption and authentication ▲ Modify an IPSec Security Policy
Completion time	35 minutes
Precautions	In this exercise, IPSec will be configured on the odd-numbered W2K8*xx* computer; the even-numbered W2K8*yy* computer will be used to test access to the odd-numbered computer.

■ **PART A: CREATING A NEW IPSEC FILTER ACTION**

1. Press Ctrl+Alt+Delete on the W2K8*xx* Windows Server 2008 computer assigned to you, and log on as the default administrator of the local computer. Your username will be Administrator. The password will be MSPress#1 or the password that your instructor or lab proctor assigns to you.

2. If the Initial Configuration Tasks (ICT) screen window opens automatically, place a checkmark next to Do not show this window at logon, and click Close.

3. Click Start, key **gpedit.msc**, and press Enter.

4. The Local Group Policy Editor window appears. Drill down to Computer Configuration→Windows Settings→Security Settings→IP Security Policies on Local Computer.

5. Right-click IP Security Policies on Local Computer, and click Manage IP filter lists and filter actions.

6. Click the Manage Filter Actions tab, click Add, and then click Next.

7. The Filter Action Name screen appears. In the Name: text box, enter **Secure-Traffic**. Click Next.

8. The Filter Action General Options screen appears. Select the Negotiate security radio button, and click Next.

9. The Communicating with Computers that Do Not Support IPSec screen appears. Select the Do not allow unsecured communications radio button, and click Next.

10. The IP Traffic Security screen appears. Accept the default selection, and click Next. Click Finish, and then click Close.

11. Remain logged on to the W2K8*xx* computer for the next section.

■ PART B: MODIFYING AN IPSEC RULE

1. Right-click Lab 9 IPSec Rule, and click Properties.

2. Click Edit. Select the Filter Action tab.

3. Click the Secure-Traffic radio button. Click OK twice.

4. Right-click Lab 9 IPSec Policy, and click Assign.

5. Remain logged on to the W2K8*xx* computer for the next section.

■ PART C: CONFIGURING A PRE-SHARED KEY AUTHENTICATION METHOD

NOTE	*The use of a pre-shared key as an IPSec authentication method is not recommended in a production network; we are configuring it here as an example only in the lab environment.*

1. Log on to the even-numbered computer as a local administrator.

Question 9	*Are you able to ping the IP address of the odd-numbered computer? Why or why not?*

2. Log off of the even-numbered computer.

3. Return to the odd-numbered computer. Right-click Lab 9 IPSec Rule, and click Properties, followed by Edit.

4. Select the Authentication Methods tab.

Question 10	What authentication method(s) is/are currently configured?

5. Click Add. The New Authentication Method Properties screen appears.

6. Click the Use this string (pre-shared key) radio button. In the text box, enter **Lab9,** and click OK.

7. Click Move up so that the new authentication method appears first in the list.

8. Highlight Kerberos. Click Remove, and then click Yes. Click OK twice to save your changes.

9. Confirm that the Lab 9 IPSec Policy on the odd-numberred computer has a value of Yes in the Assigned column, and then log off.

■ PART D: CONFIGURING A MATCHING IPSEC POLICY ON THE EVEN-NUMBERED COMPUTER

1. Log on to the even-numbered computer as a local administrator.

2. Click the Start button, key **gpedit.msc**, and press Enter.

3. The Local Group Policy Editor window opens. Browse to Computer Configuration→Windows Settings→Security Settings→IP Security Policies on Local Computer.

4. Right-click IP Security Policies on Local Computer, click Create IP Security Policy…, and then click Next.

5. In the Name: text box, enter **Lab 9 IPSec Policy**. Click Next twice, and then click Finish.

6. Click Add. Click Next three times.

7. On the IP Filter screen, click Add. In the Name: text box, enter **Lab 9 IP Filter List**.

8. Click Add. Click Next five times, followed by Finish. Click OK.

9. On the IP Filter List screen, select the Lab 9 IP Filter List radio button, and click Next.

10. The Filter Action screen appears. Click Add, followed by Next.

11. In the Name: field, enter **Secure-Traffic**. Click Next four times, and then click Finish.

12. On the Filter Action screen, select the Secure-Traffic radio button, and click Next.

13. The Authentication Method screen appears. Click the Use this string to protect the key exchange (pre-shared key) radio button. Key **Lab9** exactly as you did on the odd-numbered computer in Step 6 of Part C.

14. Click Next, click Finish, and then click OK.

15. Right-click Lab 9 IPSec Policy, and click Assign.

16. Open a command prompt window.

Question 11	*Are you able to ping the IP address of the odd-numbered computer? Why or why not?*

17. Log on to the odd-numbered computer as a local administrator. Open a command prompt window.

Question 12	*Are you able to ping the IP address of the even-numbered computer? Why or why not?*

18. Un-assign the Lab 9 IPSec Policy on both the even- and odd-numbered computers.

19. Log off of both computers.

Exercise 9.3	Configuring the Windows Firewall
Overview	You have finished testing the capacities of IPSec to secure traffic between Windows Server 2008 computers. You will now test the configuration of the Windows Firewall in Windows Server 2008.
Outcomes	After completing this exercise, you will know how to: ▲ Configure the Windows Firewall ▲ Create a Windows Firewall exception
Completion time	30 minutes
Precautions	This exercise will be completed using both the even- and odd-numbered computers. Part A of this exercise will reset the Windows Firewall to its default settings to ensure that previous exercises have not modified its default behavior.

■ PART A: RESETTING THE WINDOWS FIREWALL TO DEFAULTS

1. Log on to the W2K8*zz* computer.

2. Click Start→Control Panel. Double-click Windows Firewall.

3. The Windows Firewall applet appears. Click Change settings.

4. Click the Advanced tab. Click Restore defaults, then click Yes, and then click OK.

5. Close the Windows Firewall applet window, and then close the Windows Control Panel.

Question 13	*Are you able to ping the remote computer? That is, if you are logged on to the odd-numbered computer, are you able to ping the even-numbered computer and vice versa?*

6. Open Windows Explorer. Attempt to browse to the c$ share on the remote computer by keying **W2K8***zz***c$** and pressing Enter. For example, if you are logged on to the odd-numbered computer, key \\**W2K8***yy***c$**, and press Enter. If you are logged on to the even-numbered computer, key **W2K8***xx***c$**, and press Enter.

Question 14	*Are you able to browse to the c$ share on the remote computer?*

7. Remain logged on to the W2K8*zz* computer for the next section.

■ PART B: CREATING TEST FILE SHARES

1. Create a folder called "Lab9" in the root of the C:\ drive.

2. Share the folder as \\W2K8*zz*\Lab9 as described in Lab 6. Grant EVERYONE Reader rights to the share.

3. When prompted, configure the lab network as a private network.

4. Remain logged on to the W2K8*zz* computer for the next section.

■ PART C: TESTING WINDOWS SERVER 2008 NETWORK LOCATIONS

1. Attempt to browse to the Lab9 share on your partner's computer. From the even-numbered computer, attempt to browse to \\W2K8*xx*\Lab9; from the odd-numbered computer, attempt to browse to \\W2K8*yy*\Lab9.

Question 15	*Are you able to ping your partner's computer? Why or why not?*

Question 16	*Are you able to browse to the Lab9 share?*

2. Click Start→Control Panel. Double-click Network and Sharing Center. Click Customize.

3. The Set Network Location screen appears. In the Location type: radio button, click Public. Click Next, and then click Close. Open a command prompt.

NOTE

You must complete Step 3 on both computers before answering Questions 17 and 18!

Question 17

Are you able to ping the remote computer? Why or why not?

Question 18

Are you able to browse to the Lab9 share?

■ PART D: CREATING A WINDOWS FIREWALL EXCEPTION

1.   Click Start→Control Panel. Double-click Windows Firewall. Click Change Settings.

2.   Select the Exceptions tab. Place a checkmark next to File and Printer Sharing. Click OK.

Question 19

Are you able to browse to the Lab9 share?

3.   Log off of the W2K8*zz* computer.

Exercise 9.4	Configuring Connection Security Rules
Overview	You have finished testing IPSec rules and the Windows Firewall on a Windows Server 2008 computer. You now wish to test the new Connection Security Rules functionality within Windows Server 2008.
Outcomes	After completing this exercise, you will know how to: ▲ Create and configure a Connection Security Rule ▲ Monitor the status of the Windows Firewall
Completion time	30 minutes
Precautions	Parts A and C of this exercise will be completed on both the odd- and even-numbered computers. Part B of this exercise will only be completed on the even-numbered computer. This exercise assumes that you have completed Exercise 9.3 successfully. As in the previous exercise, we will be configuring the Connection Security Rule to use a pre-shared key, which is not a security best practice. In a production environment, Connection Security Rules should be configured using Active Directory and/or a Public Key Infrastructure (PKI).

■ PART A: CONFIGURING A CONNECTION SECURITY RULE

1. Log on to the W2K8zz computer as the local administrator.

2. Click Start→Administrative Tools→Windows Firewall with Advanced Security.

3. Click Connection Security Rules, then right-click Connection Security Rules, and click New Rule….

4. The Rule Type screen appears. Confirm that the Isolation radio button is selected, and click Next.

5. The Requirements screen appears. Select the Require authentication for inbound and outbound connections radio button, and click Next.

6. The Authentication Method screen appears.

Question 20	*What are the available authentication methods from which to choose?*

7. Select the Advanced radio button. Click Customize.

8. The Custom Advanced Authentication Methods screen appears. In the First Authentication section, click Add.

9. The First Authentication Method screen appears. Click Select the Preshared key (not recommended) radio button. In the text box, key **Lab9**. Click OK twice.

10. Click Next twice.

11. The Name screen appears. In the Name: text box, key **Lab 9 Connection Security Rule**, and then click Finish.

12. Open a command prompt window.

NOTE	*You must complete Steps 11 and 12 on both computers before answering Question 21.*

Question 21	*Are you able to ping your partner's computer?*

13. Log off of the W2K8*zz* computer.

■ PART B: SIMULATING AN UNAUTHENTICATED CONNECTION FROM THE W2K8*YY* COMPUTER

1. Log on to the even-numbered W2K8*yy* computer. Click Start→Administrative Tools→Windows Firewall with Advanced Security.

2. Click Connection Security Rules. In the right-hand pane, right-click Lab 9 Connection Security Rule, and click Properties.

3. Click the Authentication tab. In the Method section, click Customize.

4. The Customize Advanced Authentication Method screen appears. Select the Pre-shared key method that you configured in Part A, and click Edit.

5. Delete the Lab9 text, and key **BadAuthentication**. Click OK three times.

Question 22	*Are you able to ping the odd-numbered W2K8xx computer? Why or why not?*

6. Repeat Steps 1-5, and replace the BadAuthentication text with the correct pre-shared key by entering **Lab9**.

Question 23	*Are you able to ping the odd-numbered W2K8xx computer? Why or why not?*

7. Log off of the W2K8*yy* computer.

■ PART C: MONITORING THE WINDOWS FIREWALL

1. Log on to the W2K8*zz* computer. Click Start→Administrative Tools→Windows Firewall with Advanced Security.

2. Click Monitoring→Security Associations→Main Mode.

Question 24	*What Main Mode Association(s) are present?*

3. Log off of the W2K8*zz* computer.

Exercise 9.5	Configuring the Windows Firewall on Server Core (optional)
Overview	You have finished testing IPSec rules and the Windows Firewall on a full installation of Windows Server 2008. You now wish to test the configuration of Windows Firewall on a Server Core computer.
Outcomes	After completing this exercise, you will know how to: ▲ Use the netsh utility to manage the Windows Firewall ▲ Monitor the status of the Windows Firewall
Completion time	30 minutes
Precautions	This exercise will be completed on the CORE*xx* Server Core computer and the odd-numbered W2K8*xx* computer. If you skip this exercise and/or the Lab Challenge, you must still complete the Lab Cleanup Exercise before moving on to Lab 10.

■ PART A: CREATING A FILE SHARE TO TEST FIREWALL CONFIGURATION

1. Log on to the CORE*xx* Server Core computer as the local administrator.

2. At the command prompt, key **cd **, and press Enter to change directories to the root of the C:\ drive.

3. At the command prompt, key **md Lab9**, and press Enter to create the C:\Lab9 folder.

4. At the command prompt, key **net share Lab9=C:\Lab9 /GRANT:EVERYONE,READ**, and press Enter to create the \\CORE*xx*\Lab9 share. Key **shutdown /l**, and press Enter to log off of the CORE*xx* computer.

5. Log on to the W2K8*xx* computer as the local administrator.

6. Open a command prompt window.

Question 25	Are you able ping the CORExx computer?

7. Attempt to browse to \\CORE*xx*\Lab9.

Question 26	Are you able to access the file share on the Server Core computer?

8. Log off of the W2K8*xx* computer.

■ PART B: ENABLING EXCEPTIONS IN THE WINDOWS FIREWALL

1. Log on to the CORE*xx* Server Core computer as the local administrator.

2. To enable the File and Printer sharing exception in the Windows Firewall, at the command prompt, key **netsh firewall set service FILEANDPRINT**, and press Enter.

3. Key **shutdown /l**, and press Enter to log off of the CORE*xx* computer.

4. Log on to the W2K8*xx* computer as the local administrator.

5. Open a command prompt window.

Question 27	Are you able ping the CORExx computer?

6. Attempt to browse to \\CORE*xx*\Lab9.

Question 28	Are you able to access the file share on the Server Core computer?

7. Log off of the W2K8*xx* computer.

LAB REVIEW QUESTIONS

Completion time	15 minutes

1. In your own words, describe what you learned by completing this lab.

2. Why did you not need to configure a separate Windows Firewall exception to allow ping traffic when you enabled the file and printer sharing exception?

3. What filter actions are available to you when you are creating an IPSec policy?

4. In a non-Active Directory environment, what options are available to secure IPSec traffic between computers?

LAB CHALLENGE: CONFIGURING THE REMOTE ADMINISTRATION EXCEPTION

Completion time	30 minutes

You want to configure the Windows Firewall to allow you to remotely manage a Windows Server 2008 computer from an administrative console, including opening the Computer Management and Services MMC.

After completing this exercise, you will know how to:

▲ Reset the Windows Firewall configuration

▲ Configure and test the Remote Administration and Remote Desktop exceptions

Precautions: If you do not complete the Lab Challenge exercises, you must still complete the Lab Cleanup steps prior to continuing on to Lab 10.

Reset the configuration of the Windows Firewall to its default settings. Then configure an exception to allow incoming Remote Desktop and Remote Administration traffic from your partner's computer. Test the exception by connecting to your partner's computer with the Computer Management MMC, as well as connecting via the Remote Desktop Client.

> **NOTE** *If you are working in pairs, be sure to communicate with your partner so that you are not "kicking each other off" of your computers as you test the Remote Desktop exception!*

LAB CLEANUP

Completion time	30 minutes

You have completed testing of IPSec and the Windows Firewall and now need to reset your Windows Server 2008 computers to their original state prior to performing testing of additional infrastructure services that you are planning to deploy to your production network.

After completing this exercise, you will know how to:

▲ Delete IPSec Policies, filter lists, and filter actions

▲ Delete Connection Security Rules

▲ Reset the Windows Firewall to a default configuration

■ PART A: REMOVING IPSEC POLICIES, FILTER ACTIONS, AND FILTER LISTS

1. Log on to the W2K8*zz* computer as the local administrator.

2. Click the Start button, key **gpedit.msc**, and press Enter.

3. Expand Computer Configuration→Windows Settings→Security Settings→IP Security Policies on Local Computer.

4. Right-click IP Security Policies on Local Computer, and click Manage IP Filter Lists and Filter Actions.

5. On the Manage IP Filter Lists tab, highlight select the Lab 9 IP Filter List, and click Remove. Click Yes to confirm.

6. Select the Manage Filter Actions tab. Highlight the Block-Traffic filter action, and click Remove. Click Yes to confirm.

7. Repeat Step 6 to remove the Block-Traffic and Secure-Traffic filter actions.

8. Click OK to return to the Local Group Policy Editor. Right-click Lab 9 IPSec Policy, and click Delete. Click Yes to confirm.

9. Close the Local Group Policy Editor.

■ PART B: REMOVING CONNECTION SECURITY RULES

1. Click Start→Administrative Tools→Windows Firewall with Advanced Security.

2. Browse to Connection Security Rules.

3. Right-click Lab 9 Connection Security Rule, and click Delete. Click Yes to confirm.

4. Close the Windows Firewall with Advanced Security MMC.

■ **PART C: RESETTING WINDOWS FIREWALL TO THE DEFAULT CONFIGURATION**

1.   Click Start→Control Panel. Double-click Windows Firewall.

2.   Click Change Settings. On the Advanced tab, click Restore Defaults.

3.   Click OK. Close the Windows Firewall applet.

4.   Log off of the W2K8*zz* computer.

LAB 10
CONFIGURING NETWORK HEALTH

This lab contains the following exercises and activities:

Exercise 10.1   Installing Active Directory Certificate Services

Exercise 10.2   Configuring Certificate Revocation

Exercise 10.3   Configuring Certificate Templates

Exercise 10.4   Configuring Certificate Enrollment

Exercise 10.5   Configuring Network Access Protection (NAP) (optional)

Lab Review   Questions

Lab Challenge   Testing Network Access Protection Auto-Remediation

Lab Cleanup

BEFORE YOU BEGIN

Lab 10 assumes that setup has been completed as specified in the setup document and that your computer has connectivity to other lab computers and the Internet. The required exercises in Lab 10 assume that you have completed the preparatory exercises in Labs 1 and 2.

The instructor PC is preconfigured as a domain controller in the lucernepublishing.com domain for demonstration purposes and is named INSTRUCTOR01.

NOTE	*In this lab manual, you will see the characters xx, yy, and zz. These directions assume that you are working on computers configured in pairs and that each computer has a number. One number is odd, and the other number is even. For example, W2K801 is the odd-numbered computer, and W2K802 is the even-numbered computer. When you see xx, substitute the unique number assigned to the odd-numbered computer. When you see yy, substitute the unique number assigned to the even-numbered computer. When you see zz, substitute the number assigned to the computer that you are working at, either odd or even.*

The three Windows Server 2008 server computers referenced in this lab will each be configured with static IP addresses. For ease of reference, record the static IP addresses of each server that you will be working with in this lab:

INSTRUCTOR01 (Instructor Computer)

IP Address: ___.___.___.___

Subnet Mask: ___.___.___.___

Default Gateway: ___.___.___.___

W2K8*xx*: (For example: W2K801)

IP Address: ___.___.___.___

Subnet Mask: ___.___.___.___

Default Gateway: ___.___.___.___

W2K8*yy*: (For example: W2K802)

IP Address: ___.___.___.___

Subnet Mask: ___.___.___.___

Default Gateway: ___.___.___.___

If you perform the optional NAP exercise, you will also require a DHCP scope. For ease of reference, record the DHCP scope here:

DHCP Scope Start Address: ___.___.___.___

DHCP Scope End Address: ___.___.___.___

DHCP Scope Subnet Mask: ___.___.___.___

> NOTE
>
> *If students are working in pairs, exercises 10.1–10.4 can be performed on both the odd- and even-numbered computers. If students are working individually, exercises 10.1–10.4 can be performed on the odd-numbered computer only.*

SCENARIO

You are a network administrator for Trey Research. To increase security within the Trey Research network, you have decided to implement PKI certificates to allow for secure communications with internal applications, such as intranet web servers, as well as allow users to encrypt sensitive files pertaining to government exercises.

After completing this lab, you will be able to:

- Install and configure Active Directory Certificate Services

- Configure enrollment and revocation of PKI certificates

- Configure Network Access Protection

Estimated lab time: 225 minutes

> NOTE
>
> *A number of the exercises in this lab are performed on the odd-numbered computer only. To gain the most exposure to working with Active Directory Certificate Services, students can take turns or work together whenever the lab calls for work to be done on the even-numbered computer.*

Exercise 10.1	Installing Active Directory Certificate Services
Overview	To begin your deployment of Active Directory Certificate Services, you decide to deploy an enterprise root CA on a member server in your Active Directory domain.
Outcomes	After completing this exercise, you will know how to: ▲ Join a Windows Server 2008 computer to an Active Directory domain ▲ Install the Active Directory Certificate Services role on a Windows Server 2008 member server
Completion time	30 minutes
Precautions	This exercise should only be performed on the odd-numbered computer.

■ PART A: JOINING THE ODD-NUMBERED COMPUTER TO THE LUCERNEPUBLISHING.COM DOMAIN

1. Log on to the W2K8*xx* computer as the local Administrator.

2. Modify the network configuration of the W2K8*xx* computer to use INSTRUCTOR01 as its preferred DNS server.

3. Add the W2K8*xx* computer to the Lucernepublishing.com domain using the Administrator account in the lucernepublishing.com domain. Your username is Administrator. The password is MSPress#1 or the password that your instructor or lab proctor has assigned to you.

4. Restart the W2K8*xx* computer when prompted.

■ PART B: INSTALLING THE ACTIVE DIRECTORY CERTIFICATE SERVICES ROLE ON THE ODD-NUMBERED COMPUTER

1. Press Ctrl+Alt+Delete on the odd-numbered computer assigned to you, and log on as the default administrator of the lucernepublishing.com domain. Your username is Administrator. The password is MSPress#1 or the password that your instructor or lab proctor has assigned to you.

2. If the Server Manager console does not appear automatically, click Start→Server Manager.

3. In the left-hand pane, select Roles. In the right-hand pane, click Add Roles.

4. Click Next to dismiss the initial Welcome screen. The Select Server Roles screen appears. Place a checkmark next to Active Directory Certificate Services. Click Next.

5. The Introduction to Active Directory Certificate Services screen appears. Read the introductory information to Active Directory Certificate Services, and click Next.

6. The Select Role Services screen appears. Place a checkmark next to the Certification Authority Active Directory Certificate Services Role Service, and click Next.

7. The Specify Setup Type screen appears. Select the Enterprise CA type radio button, and click Next.

8. The Specify CA Type screen appears. Select the Root CA type radio button, and click Next.

9. The Set Up a Private Key screen appears. Select the Create a new private key radio button, and click Next.

10. The Configure Cryptography for CA screen appears. Accept the default values, and click Next.

11. The Configure CA Name screen appears. Enter **W2K8xx-CA**, and click Next.

12. The Set Validity Period screen appears. Accept the default value of 5 years, and click Next.

13. The Configure Certificate Database screen appears. Accept the default values, and click Next.

14. The Confirm Installation Selections screen appears. Read the confirmation information to prepare for the installation. Click Install to install the AD Certificate Services role.

15. The Installation Results screen appears. Click Close.

16. Log off of the odd-numbered computer.

Exercise 10.2	Configuring Certificate Revocation
Overview	Before you can begin to deploy public key infrastructure (PKI) certificates in a production environment, you need to configure certificate revocation so that your Active Directory Certificate Services (AD CS) infrastructure can react appropriately to certificates that need to be revoked because an employee resigns, is terminated, or encounters a situation in which their existing private key becomes stolen or otherwise compromised.
Outcomes	After completing this exercise, you will know how to: ▲ Configure Certificate Revocation on an Active Directory Certificate Services server
Completion time	30 minutes
Precautions	This exercise will be performed on the odd-numbered computer.

■ PART A: INSTALLING THE ONLINE RESPONDER

1. Log on to the odd-numbered computer as the default administrator of the lucernepublishing.com domain.

2. Click the Start button, and then click Server Manager. Drill down to Roles→Active Directory Certificate Services. Right-click Active Directory Certificate Services, and select Add Role Services.

3. Place a checkmark next to Online Responder. The Add Role Services screen appears, indicating that you need to install several IIS components to install the Online Responder. Click Add Required Role Services, and then click Next to continue.

4. The Introduction to Web Server (IIS) screen appears. Read the informational message concerning the installation of the Web Server role, and click Next.

5. The Select Role Services screen appears. Accept the default IIS features to install, and click Next.

6. The Confirm Installation Selections screen appears. Click Install to install the Online Responder role service.

7. The Installation Progress screen appears. After a few minutes, the installation will complete. Click Close when prompted.

8. Remain logged on to the odd-numbered computer for the next part of the exercise.

■ PART B: CONFIGURING THE ONLINE RESPONDER

1. In the left-hand pane within Server Manager, drill down to Roles→Active Directory Certificate Services→Certificate Templates. (If the Certificate Templates node does not appear automatically, close and re-open the Server Manager console, and try again.)

2. Right-click the OCSP Response Signing template, and click Properties.

3. Select the Security tab. Click Add. The Select Users, Computers, or Groups screen appears. Click Object Types, place a checkmark next to Computers, and then click OK. Key **W2K8xx**, and then click OK. Place a checkmark next to Enroll as well as Autoenroll under the Allow column, and then click OK.

4. Right-click the Certificate Templates folder. Expand the W2K8xx-CA node, and click New→Certificate Template to Issue. Select the OCSP Response Signing certificate template, and click OK.

■ PART C: ESTABLISHING A REVOCATION CONFIGURATION FOR THE CERTIFICATION AUTHORITY

1. In the left-hand pane of Server Manager, navigate to Roles→Active Directory Certificate Services→Online Responder: W2K8xx→Revocation Configuration.

2. Right-click Revocation Configuration, and click Add Revocation Configuration.

3. The Getting Started with Adding a Revocation Configuration Screen appears. Read the information on the Getting Started screen, and then click Next.

4. The Name the Revocation Configuration screen appears. Enter **W2K8xx-CA-REV**, and click Next.

5. The Select CA Certificate Location screen appears. Ensure that the Select a certificate for an Existing enterprise CA radio button is selected, and click Next.

6. The Choose CA Certificate screen appears. Confirm that the Browse CA certificates published in Active Directory screen is selected, and then click Browse.

7. The Select Certification Authority screen appears. Confirm that the W2K8xx-CA certificate is selected, and then click OK. Click Next to continue.

8. The Select Signing Certificate screen appears. Confirm that the Automatically select a signing certificate radio button is selected. Confirm that there is a checkmark next to Auto-enroll for an OCSP signing certificate. Confirm that the W2K8*xx*-CA certificate is selected based on the OCSPResponseSigning template.

9. Click Next, and then click Finish to configure the Revocation Configuration.

10. Navigate to W2K8*xx*-CA→Issued Certificates. Confirm that an OCSP Response Signing Certificate has been issued to the Certification Authority.

11. Log off of the odd-numbered computer.

Exercise 10.3	Configuring Certificate Templates
Overview	Now that you have installed the Active Directory Certificate Services role and configured certificate revocation, you decide to deploy certificate templates that will allow Web server certificates to be deployed across your Active Directory network. Because your clients and servers are all running Windows XP, Windows Vista, Windows Server 2003, or Windows Server 2008, you wish to configure templates that allow for certificate auto-enrollment to ease the process of deploying certificates to your users and computers.
Outcomes	After completing this exercise, you will know how to: ▲ Configure PKI certificate templates ▲ Publish certificate templates on a Windows Server 2008 CA
Completion time	30 minutes
Precautions	This exercise will be performed on the odd-numbered computer only.

■ PART A: CONFIGURING A WEB SERVER CERTIFICATE TEMPLATE

1. Log on to the odd-numbered computer as the default administrator of the lucernepublishing.com domain.

2. Click Start, followed by Server Manager. In the left-hand pane, expand the Roles node followed by the Active Directory Certificate Services node.

3. Right-click the Web Server template, and click Properties.

4. Select the Security tab. Click Add. The Select Users, Computers, or Groups screen appears. Click Object Types, place a checkmark next to Computers, and then click OK. Key **W2K8xx**, and then click OK. Place a checkmark next to Enroll under the Allow column, and then click OK.

5. Right-click the Web server Server template, and choose Duplicate Template.

6. The Duplicate Template screen appears, prompting you for the minimum operating system version that should be supported by this template. Select Windows Server 2008, Enterprise Edition, and click OK.

7. The Properties of New Template window is displayed. On the General tab, key **W2K8xx-WebServer-Cert** in the Template Display Name text box. Confirm that there is a checkmark next to Publish certificate in Active Directory; add a checkmark here if it is not already present.

8. Select the Security tab.

9. Click Add. The Select Users, Computers, or Groups screen appears. Click Object Types, place a checkmark next to Computers, and then click OK. Key **W2K8xx**, and then click OK. Place a checkmark next to Enroll and Autoenroll under the Allow column.

10. Select the Superseded Templates tab. Click Add. The Add Superseded Templates screen appears. Select the built-in Web Server certificate template, and then click OK.

11. Click OK.

■ PART B: CONFIGURING THE CA TO ISSUE CERTIFICATES FOR EACH TEMPLATE

1. In the left-hand pane, expand W2K8xx-CA.

2. Right-click the Certificate Templates folder, and click New→Certificate Template to Issue.

3. The Enable Certificate Templates screen appears. Click W2K8xx-Webserver-Cert, and click OK.

4. Log off of the odd-numbered computer.

Exercise 10.4	Configuring Certificate Enrollment
Overview	You have determined that your Active Directory Certificate Services infrastructure is ready to be placed into production use on your network. To do this, you now need to configure your user and computer accounts to allow for PKI certificate auto-enrollment. For those certificate types that do not allow for auto-enrollment, you need to use manual request mechanisms to obtain certificates for the appropriate users and computers.
Outcomes	After completing this exercise, you will know how to: ▲ Install the Certificate Services Web Enrollment service ▲ Request PKI certificates manually using the Certificate Services Web Enrollment service
Completion time	30 minutes
Precautions	This exercise should be performed on the odd-numbered computer.

■ PART A: INSTALLING THE CERTIFICATION AUTHORITY WEB ENROLLMENT ROLE SERVICE

1. Log on to the odd-numbered computer as the default administrator of the lucernepublishing.com domain.

2. Click the Start button, and then click Server Manager. Drill down to Roles→Active Directory Certificate Services. Right-click Active Directory Certificate Services, and select Add Role Services.

3. Place a checkmark next to Certification Authority Web Enrollment. The Add Required Features screen appears, indicating that you need to install additional IIS components to install the Certification Authority Web Enrollment role service. Click Add Required Features, and then click Next to continue.

4. The Introduction to Web Server (IIS) screen appears. Read the informational message concerning the installation of the Web Server role, and click Next.

5. The Select Role Services screen appears. Accept the default IIS features to install, and click Next.

6. The Confirm Installation Selections screen appears. Click Install to install the Certification Authority Web Enrollment role service.

7. The Installation Progress screen appears. After a few minutes, the installation will complete. Click Close when prompted.

■ PART B: REQUESTING A WEB SERVER CERTIFICATE FOR THE ODD-NUMBERED COMPUTER

1. Click the Start button, click Administrative Tools, and then click Internet Information Services (IIS) Manager.

2. The Internet Information Services (IIS) Manager page will appear. In the left-hand pane, double-click the W2K8*xx* node.

3. The W2K8*xx* Home screen will appear in the main pane. Scroll down through the IIS section, and double-click the Server Certificates icon. In the right-hand pane, click Create Domain Certificate.

4. The Distinguished Name (DN) Properties screen appears. Enter the following information, and then click Next:

   - Common name: **W2K8*xx*.lucernepublishing.com**

   - Organization: **lucernepublishing.com**

   - Organizational unit: **HQ**

   - City/locality: **Redmond**

   - State/province: **WA**

   - Country/region: **US**

5. The Online Certification Authority screen appears. Click Select next to the Specify Online Certification Authority text box. The Select Certification Authority screen is displayed. Select W2K8*xx*-CA, and click OK. In the Friendly Name text box, enter **w2k8*xx*.lucernepublishing.com**, and click Finish.

■ PART C: ENABLING SSL CONNECTIONS ON THE ODD-NUMBERED COMPUTER

1. In the left-hand pane of IIS Manager, expand W2K8*xx*, and then expand the Sites node.

2. Right-click Default Web Site, and choose Edit Bindings.

3. The Site Bindings screen appears. Click Add.

4. The Add Site Binding screen appears. In the Type drop-down box, select https. In the SSL Certificate drop-down box, select w2k8*xx*.lucernepublishing.com.

5. Click OK, and then click Close.

6. In the left-hand pane of IIS Manager, drill down to the Default Web Site→CertSrv node; double-click CertSrv. In the right-hand center pane, scroll down, and double-click SSL Settings.

7. Place a checkmark next to Require SSL, and then click Apply in the Actions pane.

8. Log off of the odd-numbered computer.

Exercise 10.5 (optional)	Configuring Network Access Protection (NAP)
Overview	One concern voiced by management has been that surrounding users lose the private keys associated with their PKI certificates. After consulting with management and key members of the Trey Research staff, you determine that it will not be sufficient to simply instruct users to back up their private keys on an individual basis. Accordingly, you decide to configure key archival on your Certificate Services server to allow administrators to recover private keys that become lost or are otherwise unavailable.
Outcomes	After completing this exercise, you will know how to: ▲ Install and configure the DHCP Server Service ▲ Install and configure Network Access Protection
Completion time	40 minutes
Precautions	This exercise should be performed on the odd-numbered computer. If you do not complete the optional exercise and/or the Lab Challenge, you must still perform the Lab Cleanup exercise before continuing to Lab 11.

■ PART A: INSTALLING THE DHCP SERVER SERVICE ON THE ODD-NUMBERED W2K8XX COMPUTER

1. Log on to the odd-numbered computer as the default administrator of the lucernepublishing.com domain.

2. In the left-hand pane of Server Manager, double-click Roles.

3. Click Add Roles. Click Next to dismiss the initial Welcome screen.

4. The Select Server Roles screen appears. Place a checkmark next to DHCP Server, and then click Next.

5. The Introduction to DHCP Server screen appears. Click Next. If the Network Connection Bindings screen appears, click Next to continue.

6. The Specify IPv4 DNS Server Settings screen appears. Enter **lucernepublishing.com** as the parent domain. Enter the IP address of **INSTRUCTOR01** as the preferred DNS server. Click Next.

7. The Specify IPv4 WINS Server Settings screen appears. Confirm that the WINS is not required for applications on this network radio button is selected, and click Next.

8. The Add or Edit DHCP Scopes screen appears. Click Add.

9. The Add Scope screen appears. Enter the following information, and click OK.

   - Scope Name: **Lab 10 Exercise 10-5 Scope**

   - Starting IP Address: The starting IP address that has been assigned by your instructor or lab proctor

   - Ending IP Address: The ending IP address that has been assigned by your instructor or lab proctor

   - Subnet Mask: The subnet mask that has been assigned by your instructor or lab proctor

   - Default Gateway: The default gateway that has been assigned by your instructor or lab proctor

   - Subnet Type: **Wired**

Question 1	*What is the default lease duration of a Wired subnet type?*

10. Click Next. The Configure DHCPv6 Stateless Mode screen appears.

11. Click Next. The Specify IPv6 DNS Server Settings screen appears. Delete any values that have been pre-populated, and click Next.

12. The Authorize DHCP Server screen appears. Provide the credentials for the default administrator of the lucernepublishing.com domain, and click Next.

13. Click Install, and then click Close.

14. Remain logged on to the W2K8*xx* computer for the next section.

■ PART B: INSTALLING THE NETWORK POLICY SERVICE ROLE ON THE ODD-NUMBERED COMPUTER

1. In the left-hand pane of Server Manager, double-click Roles.

2. Click Add Roles. Click Next to dismiss the initial Welcome screen.

3. The Select Server Roles screen appears. Place a checkmark next to Network Policy and Access Services. Click Next twice to continue.

4. The Select Role Services screen appears. Place a checkmark next to Network Policy Server.

5. Click Next followed by Install, and then click Close.

6. Remain logged on to the W2K8*xx* computer for the next section.

■ PART C: CONFIGURING NETWORK ACCESS PROTECTION

1. Click Start→Administrative Tools→Network Policy Server.

2. In the Getting Started pane, click Configure NAP.

3. The Network Connection Method screen appears. Select Dynamic Host Configuration Protocol (DHCP) in the drop-down box, and click Next twice.

4. The Specify DHCP Scopes screen appears. Click Add…. Key **Lab 10 Exercise 5 Scope**, and click OK. Click Next.

5. The Configure User Groups and Machine Groups screen appears. Click Add Machine…. The Select Group screen appears. Key **Domain Computers**, and click OK. Click Next.

6. The Specify a NAP Remediation Server Group and URL screen appears. Click Next.

7. The Define NAP Health Policy screen appears. Click the Allow full network access to NAP-ineligible computers radio button.

Question 2	What Security Health Validator is selected by default?

8. Click Next, and then click Finish.

9. You are returned to the Network Policy Server window. Browse to Network Access Protection→System Health Validators.

10. Right-click Windows Security Health Validator, and click Properties. Click Configure.

11. On the Windows Vista tab, deselect all checkboxes except for A firewall is enabled for all network connections.

12. Click OK twice.

13. Log off of the W2K8*xx* computer.

LAB REVIEW QUESTIONS

Completion time	15 minutes

1. In your own words, describe what you learned by completing this lab.

2. Will the configuration that you established in this lab allow you to take your root CA offline for added security? Why or why not?

3. What other enforcement mechanisms are available with Network Access Protection?

4. By default, what does the Windows Security Health Validator check for on a Windows Vista client?

LAB CHALLENGE: TESTING NETWORK ACCESS PROTECTION AUTO-REMEDIATION

Completion time	20 minutes

Now that you have configured a Network Access Protection enforcement server in a test environment, you wish to test how it enforces network health for your Vista clients.

After completing this exercise, you will know how to:

▲ Join a Windows Vista computer to an Active Directory domain

▲ Test Network Access Protection auto-remediation

Precautions: If you do not perform the Lab Challenge, you must still perform the Lab Cleanup.

> **NOTE**
>
> *If there is a DHCP server running in the classroom other than the NAP enforcement servers configured in this exercise, it should be disabled for the duration of this exercise so that the Vista computer can receive its IP address from a NAP-protected DHCP server.*

1. Join the Vista*xx* computer to the lucernepublishing.com domain if it is not alread configured as a member of the domain.

2. Configure the Vista*xx* computer to receive its IP address from DHCP. Confirm that it is receiving its IP address from one of the NAP servers in the classroom if there is more than one on the same network. (If the student is working alone, this will default to the W2K8*xx* computer configured in Exercise 10.5.)

3. Open a command-prompt window, and enter **ping –t W2K8*yy*** to monitor network connectivity during this exercise.

4. Disable the Windows Firewall, and discuss the resultant behavior of the Windows Vista computer.

LAB CLEANUP

Completion time	30 minutes

In this exercise you will roll back all changes made in this lab and prepare for Lab 11.

After completing this exercise, you will know how to:

▲ Decommission a Windows Server 2008 Certificate Services server

▲ Remove Windows Server 2008 roles

■ PART A: DECOMMISSIONING THE CERTIFICATE SERVICES SERVER

1. On the odd-numbered computer, log on as the default administrator of the lucernepublishing.com domain.

2. If the Server Manager console does not appear automatically, click the Start button, and then click Server Manager.

3. Drill down to the Roles node, and click Remove roles. Click Next to dismiss the Welcome Screen.

4. The Remove Server Roles screen appears. Remove the checkmarks next to Active Directory Certificate Services, Network Policy Server (if you completed Exercise 10.5), DHCP Server (if you completed Exercise 10.5), and Web Server (IIS). Click Next.

5. The Confirm Removal Selections screen appears. Click Remove to begin the removal process.

6. The Removal Results screen appears. Click Close, and then click Yes to restart the server.

■ PART B: DELETING PKI CERTIFICATES

1. On the odd-numbered computer, log on as the administrator of the lucernepublishing.com domain.

2. Open a blank MMC console. Add the Certificates MMC snap-in for the local computer. Browse to the Intermediate Certification Authority node.

3. Under the Certificate Revocation List folder, delete W2K8*xx*-CA.

4. Under the Certificates folder, delete W2K8*xx*-CA.

■ PART C: COMPLETING FINAL CLEANUP

1. Disjoin the W2K8*xx* and Vista*xx* (if applicable) computers from the lucernepublishing.com domain.

2. Remove the preferred DNS server setting for the W2K8*xx* computer.

LAB 11
MAINTAINING WINDOWS SERVER 2008 FILE SERVICES

This lab contains the following exercises and activities:

Exercise 11.1   Installing and Configuring Shadow Copies

Exercise 11.2   Confirming Shadow Copies Functionality

Exercise 11.3   Installing and Configuring Windows Server Backup

Exercise 11.4   Installing and Configuring Disk Quotas

Lab Review   Questions

Lab Challenge   Creating File Screens

Lab Cleanup

BEFORE YOU BEGIN

Lab 11 assumes that setup has been completed as specified in the setup document and that your computer has connectivity to other lab computers and the Internet. The required exercises in Lab 11 assume that you have completed the preparatory exercises in Labs 1 and 2. Exercise 11.3 assumes that you have a second hard drive installed in the computer you are backing up that is at least 1MB larger than the size of the installed C:\ drive. The drive should be initialized as a basic disk and formatted as a single volume before beginning Exercise 11.3.

The instructor PC is preconfigured as a domain controller in the lucernepublishing.com domain for demonstration purposes and is named INSTRUCTOR01.

> **NOTE**
>
> *In this lab manual, you will see the characters xx, yy, and zz. These directions assume that you are working on computers configured in pairs and that each computer has a number. One number is odd, and the other number is even. For example, W2K801 is the odd-numbered computer, and W2K802 is the even-numbered computer. When you see xx, substitute the unique number assigned to the odd-numbered computer. When you see yy, substitute the unique number assigned to the even-numbered computer. When you see zz, substitute the number assigned to the computer that you are working at, either odd or even.*

The Windows Server 2008 computers referenced in this lab will each be configured with static IP addresses. For ease of reference, record the static IP addresses of each server that you will be working with in this lab:

INSTRUCTOR01 (Instructor Computer)

IP Address: ___.___.___.___

Subnet Mask: ___.___.___.___

Default Gateway: ___.___.___.___

W2K8*xx*: (For example: W2K801)

IP Address: ___.___.___.___

Subnet Mask: ___.___.___.___

Default Gateway: ___.___.___.___

W2K8*yy*: (For example: W2K802)

IP Address: ___.___.___.___

Subnet Mask: ___.___.___.___

Default Gateway: ___.___.___.___

SCENARIO

You are a network administrator for Lucerne Publishing. Lucerne Publishing is in the process of deploying numerous Windows Server 2008 file servers to several remote locations. To make provisions for ongoing maintenance of file shares in remote offices, you will configure Shadow Copies of Shared Folders as well as the Windows Server Backup feature. Additionally, you will configure disk quotas to restrict disk usage on remote file servers.

NOTE	*If students are working in pairs, the exercises in this lab can be performed on both the odd- and even-numbered servers. If students are working individually, the exercises in this lab can be performed on the odd-numbered computer only.*

After completing this lab, you will be able to:

- Install and configure shadow copies

- Confirm shadow copies functionality

- Install and configure Windows Server Backup

- Install and configure disk quotas

Estimated lab time: 205 minutes

Exercise 11.1	Installing and Configuring Shadow Copies
Overview	You have finished testing multiple servers to act as file servers within your organization. You will now test the Shadow Copies of Shared Folders feature of Windows Server 2008 to allow users to restore previous versions of files and folders.
Outcomes	After completing this exercise, you will know how to: ▲ Configure shared folders ▲ Configure Shadow Copies of Shared Folders ▲ Test the functionality of Shadow Copies of Shared Folders
Completion time	30 minutes
Precautions	If students are working in pairs, the exercises in this lab can be performed on both the odd- and even-numbered servers. If students are working individually, the exercises in this lab can be performed on the odd-numbered computer only.

■ PART A: CONFIGURING A WINDOWS FILE SHARE FOR TESTING

1. Press Ctrl+Alt+Delete on the W2K8*zz* Windows Server 2008 computer assigned to you, and log on as the default administrator of the local computer. Your username will be Administrator. The password will be MSPress#1 or the password that your instructor or lab proctor assigns to you.

2. If the Initial Configuration Tasks (ICT) screen window opens automatically, place a checkmark next to Do not show this window at logon, and click Close.

3. Create a folder named **Lab11** in the root of the C:\ drive. Share the folder as \\W2K8*zz*\Lab11, and configure W2K8*zz*\Users with Co-owner permissions. If a Network discovery and file sharing window appears, click No, make the network that I am connected to a private network.

4. Create a text file within the Lab11 share named **W2K8*zz*.txt**. Edit the file to include the text **Contents of W2K8*zz* file during Part A of Exercise 11.1**. Save the changes, and close the file.

5. Remain logged on to the W2K8*zz* computer for the next section.

■ PART B: CONFIGURING SHADOW COPIES OF SHARED FOLDERS

1. Click the Start button, and then click Computer.

2. The Computer window appears. Right-click Local Disk (C:), and click Properties.

3. Click the Shadow Copies tab.

Question 1	*What is the current value in the Next Run Time column for the C:\ drive?*

4. Click Enable, and then click Yes to confirm.

Question 2	*How much space is now being used by Shadow Copies on the C:\ drive?*

5. Click Settings.

| Question 3 | What is the space limit for Shadow Copies on the C:\ drive? |

6. Click Schedule.

| Question 4 | What is the schedule for creation of Shadow Copies? |

7. Click Cancel three times.

8. Log off of the W2K8*zz* computer.

Exercise 11.2	Confirming Shadow Copies Functionality
Overview	You have finished configuring Shadow Copies of Shared Folders on a test server in your lab. You will now test the functionality of this feature within Windows Server 2008.
Outcomes	After completing this exercise, you will know how to: ▲ Restore a file using Shadow Copies of Shared Folders
Completion time	20 minutes
Precautions	If students are working in pairs, the exercises in this lab can be performed on both the odd- and even-numbered servers. If students are working individually, the exercises in this lab can be performed on the odd-numbered computer only.

■ **PART A: USING SHADOW COPIES OF SHARED FOLDERS TO RECOVER FROM AN UNWANTED CHANGE**

1. Log on to the W2K8*zz* computer as the local Administrator.

2. Open Windows Explorer. Browse to the \\w2k8*zz*\Lab11 shared folder using the UNC path. Open the W2K8*zz*.txt file, and add the following line of text: **"Text added during Part A of Exercise 11.2."**

| NOTE | *You must use the UNC path to access the Lab11 shared folder for Shadow Copies of Shared Folders to be created properly in the following steps.* |

3. Save and close the W2K8*zz*.txt file. Reopen and then close the file to confirm that your edit was successful.

4. To simulate recovering from an unwanted change, right-click the W2K8*zz*.txt file, and click Restore previous versions....

5. Click Open.

Question 5	What are the contents of the file?

6. Close the W2K8*zz*.txt file. Click Cancel.

7. Click the Start button, and click Computer. Right-click Local Disk (C:), and click Properties.

8. Click the Shadow Copies tab. Click Create Now to create a second Shadow Copy of the contents of the Lab11 share.

9. Click OK.

10. Return to the Lab11 shared folder. Right-click W2K8*zz*.txt, and click Restore Previous versions....

11. Select the newer Shadow Copy that was created. Click Open.

Question 6	What are the contents of the file?

12. Close the W2K8*zz*.txt file. Click Cancel.

13. To simulate recovering from an accidental deletion, delete the W2K8*zz*.txt file. Close the \\W2K8*zz*\Lab11 shared folder.

14. Open \\W2K8*zz* in Windows Explorer. Right-click Lab11, and click Restore Previous Versions....

15. Click the newer Shadow Copies version of the W2K8*zz*.txt file. Click Restore twice, and then click OK to confirm.

16. Click OK. Double-click the Lab11 shared folder. Confirm that the W2K8*zz*.txt file is in place and contains the contents listed in Question 6.

17. Log off of the W2K8*zz* computer.

Exercise 11.3	Installing and Configuring Windows Server Backup
Overview	You have finished testing multiple servers to act as infrastructure servers within your organization. You will now test the Windows Server Backup feature to allow you to back up and restore critical files in Windows Server 2008.
Outcomes	After completing this exercise, you will know how to: ▲ Install and configure Windows Server Backup ▲ Perform a Windows backup ▲ Create a Windows restore
Completion time	45 minutes
Precautions	If students are working in pairs, the exercises in this lab can be performed on both the odd- and even-numbered servers. If students are working individually, the exercises in this lab can be performed on the odd-numbered computer only. This exercise assumes that you have a second hard drive installed in the computer you are backing up that is at least 1MB larger than the size of the installed C:\ drive. The drive should be initialized and formatted as a single volume before beginning Exercise 11.3.

■ PART A: INSTALLING AND CONFIGURING WINDOWS SERVER BACKUP

1. Press Ctrl+Alt+Delete on the W2K8*zz* computer assigned to you, and log on as the default administrator of the local computer. Your username will be Administrator. The password will be MSPress#1 or the password that your instructor or lab proctor assigns to you.

2. If the Server Manager screen is not already open, click the Start button, and then click Server Manager. Expand the Server Manager window to full screen if necessary.

3. In the left-hand pane, select the Features node. In the right-hand pane, click Add Features.

4. The Select Features screen appears. Expand Windows Server Backup Features. Place a checkmark next to Windows Server Backup. Click Next, and then click Install.

5. Click Close when the installation completes.

6. Click Start→Administrative Tools→Windows Server Backup. The Windows Server Backup window appears. Choose Backup Once from the Action menu. The Backup Options Wizard appears. Click Next to begin performing a one-time backup.

7. If this is the first backup you have performed, you may see a warning screen describing access to earlier backups. If you receive this warning, click Yes to continue.

8. The Select backup configuration screen appears. Select the Custom radio button, and click Next.

9. The Select backup items window appears. Be sure that the second hard drive on the W2K8*zz* computer has been deselected, and then click Next.

10. The Specify destination type window appears. Select the Local drives radio button, and then click Next.

11. The Select backup destination window appears. In the backup destination drop-down box, confirm that the second hard drive on the W2K8*zz* computer is selected, and then click Next.

12. The Specify advanced option window appears. Read the description of the VSS copy backup option, and click Next.

13. The Confirmation screen appears. Click Backup to begin the backup process.

NOTE	*Depending on lab hardware, the backup may take some time to complete.*

14. Click Close when the backup completes. Close the Windows Server Backup console.

15. Remain logged on to the W2K8*zz* computer for the next section.

■ PART B: PERFORMING A RESTORE OPERATION

1. To simulate a failure of the file server, delete the Lab11 folder on the W2K8*zz* computer. Click Yes to any prompts indicating that the folder is shared, and confirm the deletion.

2. Click Start→Administrative Tools→Windows Server Backup.

3. Click Recover.... The Getting Started window appears. Ensure that the This server (W2K8*zz*) radio button is selected. Click Next.

4. The Select backup date screen appears. Select the time and date of the backup that you performed in Part B. Click Next.

5. The Select recovery type screen appears. Ensure that the Files and folders radio button is selected. Click Next.

6. The Select items to recover screen appears. Double-click W2K8*zz* in the left-hand pane. Browse to Local disk (C:). Click the Lab11 folder, and click Next.

7. The Specify recovery options screen appears. Accept the default selections, and click Next.

8. Click Recover to begin the restore operation. Click Close.

9. Open the C:\ folder, and confirm that the Lab11 folder and its contents have been restored.

Question 7	*Is the Lab11 folder shared following the restore? Why or why not?*

10. Close the Windows Server Backup window. Log off of the W2K8*zz* computer.

Exercise 11.4	Installing and Configuring Disk Quotas
Overview	Lucerne Publishing management is concerned that individual users will take up all available disk space on the file servers deployed in the remote offices. You need to test the functionality of disk quota templates and disk templates within the Windows Server 2008 File Services role.
Outcomes	After completing this exercise, you will know how to: ▲ Configure File Server Resource Manager (FSRM) disk quota templates ▲ Configure File Server Resource Manager (FSRM) disk quotas
Completion time	45 minutes
Precautions	If students are working in pairs, the exercises in this lab can be performed on both the odd- and even-numbered servers. If students are working individually, the exercises in this lab can be performed on the odd-numbered computer only.

■ PART A: ADDING THE FILE SERVER RESOURCE MANAGER ROLE SERVICE

1. Log on to the W2K8*zz* computer as the local Administrator. If the Server Manager console does not appear automatically, click Start followed by Server Manager. Expand the Server Manager to full screen if needed.

2. Click Roles→Roles, then right-click File Services, and choose Add Role Services.

3. Place a checkmark next to File Server Resource Manager. Click Next.

4. The Configure Storage Usage Monitoring screen appears. Place a checkmark next to the C:\ drive.

5. Click Next twice, and then click Install.

6. Click Close when the installation completes.

7. Remain logged on to the W2K8*zz* computer for the next section.

■ PART B: CONFIGURING DISK QUOTA TEMPLATES

1. Click Start→Administrative Tools→File Server Resource Manager.

2. The File Server Resource Manager screen appears. Drill down to Quota Management→Quota Templates.

Question 8	What quota templates are configured by default?

3. Right-click Quota Templates, and click Create Quota Template….

4. The Create Quota Template screen appears. Enter the following information, and click OK:

    - Template Name: **Lab 11 Quota Template**

    - Space Limit: **1 KB**

5. Remain logged on to the W2K8*zz* computer for the next section.

■ PART C: CONFIGURING DISK QUOTA

1. Click Quotas. Right-click Quotas, and choose Create Quota....

2. The Create Quota screen appears. In the Quota path section, click Browse.... Select the C:\Lab11 folder, and click OK.

3. In the Derive properties from this quota template (recommended): drop-down box, select Lab 11 Quota Template. Click Create.

Question 9	What percentage of the disk quota that you just configured has been used?

4. Open C:\Lab11 in Windows Explorer. Attempt to create a new file. Click Cancel when prompted.

Question 10	Are you able to create the file?

5. Right-click the quota that you created in Step 3, and click Delete. Click Yes to confirm. Return to c:\Lab11, and attempt to create a new file named **Exercise11-4.txt.**

Question 11	Are you able to create the file?

6. Log off of the W2K8*zz* computer.

LAB REVIEW QUESTIONS

Completion time   15 minutes

1. In your own words, describe what you learned by completing this lab.

2. Can disk quotas be configured if the File Server Resource Manager is not installed?

3. How are file screens enforced?

4. What is the difference between a hard quota and a soft quota?

LAB CHALLENGE: CREATING FILE SCREENS

Completion time	30 minutes

Once you have installed a Windows Server 2008 file server, you want to restrict users' ability to save different file types onto a particular server in order to save space on the server.

After completing this exercise, you will know how to:

▲ Create a file screen template

▲ Create a file screen

Precaution: If you do not complete the Lab Challenge exercise, you must still complete the Lab Cleanup steps prior to continuing on to the final Troubleshooting Lab.

Create a file screen template that prevents the storage of .MP3 and .AVI files on a Windows Server 2008 file server. Then create a file screen that will enforce this restriction.

LAB CLEANUP

Completion time	20 minutes

You have completed testing of Windows file server functions and now need to reset your Windows Server 2008 computers to their original state prior to deploying the servers into a production environment.

After completing this exercise, you will know how to:

▲ Remove the File Server Role

1. Unshare and delete the Lab11 folder and its contents.

2. Remove the Windows Server Backup feature from the W2K8*zz* computer.

3. Remove the File Services role from the W2K8*zz* computer. Restart the computer when prompted.

TROUBLESHOOTING LAB
DEPLOYING NETWORK SERVICES

■ **PART A: REVIEWING A NETWORK**

In this portion of the Troubleshooting Lab, you are the network administrator for City Power & Light (http://www.cpandl.com). City Power & Light has five different locations named Central, Northwest, Northeast, Southwest, and Southeast. The Central location has 500 client computers and two network servers. The Northwest and Northeast locations have approximately 75 client computers and one server computer each. The Southwest and Southeast locations have 100 client computers and one network server each. Figure 1 illustrates the company's network infrastructure. Each location is configured as a separate IPv4 subnet, with a router configured at each location to provide access to other internal network locations as well as access to the Internet.

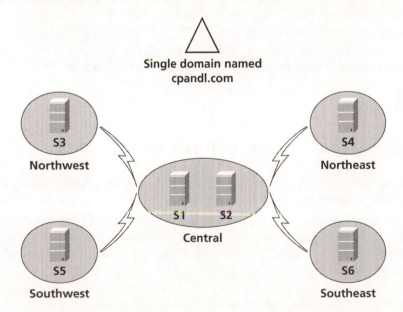

Figure 1
City Power & Light network infrastructure

S1, S2, S3, S4, S5, and S6 are servers on the City Power & Light network. All of these servers run Windows Server 2008, Standard Edition. All client computers run Windows Vista, Enterprise Edition. All computers are configured in a single workgroup named WORKGROUP.

Andy Ruth, director of City Power & Light, asks you to design a DHCP and DNS infrastructure for the company. He wants all Vista clients to obtain their IP addresses automatically, and he needs all workstation and server computers to have name resolution capabilities to every server in the network. He tells you that all users use the same applications and have roughly equivalent configurations. He thinks that the 56-Kbps links are a little slow for the company, and he wants to have control over the traffic sent across those links. However, he says that the T-1 links can handle more traffic without a problem. Andy tells you that there are no special security requirements that would require isolating any of the remote locations from the central location.

Based on what you know about the City Power & Light network infrastructure, answer each of the following questions.

1. How many DHCP servers should you configure for the CP and L network, and where should they reside?

2. How many DNS servers should you configure for the CP and L network, and where should they reside?

3. At a minimum, which DHCP options should you assign?

4. You have decided to deploy DNS servers to the Northwest and Northeast locations, and you have deployed secondary DNS zones to each server. CP and L IT management is concerned about controlling the amount of DNS traffic that is sent over internal WAN links, as these links are already heavily utilized. What feature of Windows DNS will allow you to minimize the amount of name resolution traffic that is sent over the WAN?

■ PART B: DEPLOYING MULTIPLE NETWORK SERVICES

To experiment with DHCP, DNS, and IPSec within a networked environment, you want to configure a test network that will be used to install and configure DHCP and DNS. This test network will be configured with an IP subnet of 192.168.0.0/24. This test environment will consist of one computer that is running the DHCP and DNS server services and one computer that is used to test those services in addition to IPSec. Students can work in pairs or individually using two computers per student.

Your deployment should include the following tasks:

- Install and deploy a DHCP server on a Microsoft Windows Server 2008 computer.

- Configure a DHCP server to respond to IP address lease requests.

- Configure a DHCP server to give out the appropriate IP addressing scope options.

- Install and deploy a DNS server infrastructure on a computer that runs Windows Server 2008.

- Secure traffic between the two computers using a pre-shared key of "TroubleshootingLab."

When you are finished, be prepared to demonstrate to your instructor that your servers can:

- Communicate using Transmission Control Protocol/Internet Protocol (TCP/IP).

- Receive dynamic IP addressing information through DHCP.

- Communicate using the DNS Server service to resolve internal child domain host names.

- Communicate securely using a pre-shared key with IPSec.

■ PART C: TROUBLESHOOTING

In this portion of the Troubleshooting Lab, you are assigned to resolve a communication problem introduced by the instructor after the completion of Part B. As you proceed with the troubleshooting process, documenting the processes you use to fix the problem is crucial to your overall success. Record the steps and troubleshooting processes, and include information such as the following:

- What did you look at to diagnose the problem? List the steps you took to diagnose the problem, even those that didn't work.

- What was the problem you discovered? What was the cause of the problem?

- What was the solution? What steps did you take to resolve the problem?

- What tests did you perform to confirm the problem's resolution, and what were the results of those tests?

- List the resources you used to help solve the problem.

The malfunctions introduced on the networks are designed to inhibit communications in some way—either between the computers in the child domain or between domain computers and the other domains in the classroom. You can use the Ping utility, Tracert utility, Nslookup utility, Dnscmd utility, IPconfig, utility, or any other utilities to test the connections and help troubleshoot the problem.